PHRASE
TU

C000079614

PHRASEBOOK AA
TURKISH

English edition prepared by First Edition Translations Ltd,
Great Britain
Designed and produced by AA Publishing
First published in 1992 as Wat & Hoe Turks,
© Uitgeverij Kosmos bv - Utrecht/Antwerpen
Van Dale Lexicografie bv - Utrecht/Antwerpen
This edition © Automobile Association Developments Limited 2006
Reprinted September 2008

A CIP catalogue record for this book is available from the
British Library.

Published by AA Publishing (a trading name of Automobile
Association Developments Limited, whose registered office is
Fanum House, Basingstoke, Hampshire RG21 4EA. Registered
number 1878835).

Typeset by Kate Harling.
Printed and bound in China by Everbest.

Find out more about AA Publishing by visiting our website at
www.theAA.com/bookshop

A03953

Contents

Introduction

● **Welcome to the AA's essential Phrase Books series**, covering the most popular European languages and containing everything you'd expect from a comprehensive language series. They're concise, accessible and easy to understand, and you'll find them indispensable on your trip abroad.

Each guide is divided into 15 themed sections and starts with a pronunciation table which gives you the phonetic spelling to all the words and phrases you'll need to know for your trip, while at the back of the book is an extensive word list and grammar guide which will help you construct basic sentences in your chosen language.

Throughout the book you'll come across coloured boxes with a 🔲 beside them. These are designed to help you if you can't understand what your listener is saying to you. Hand the book over to them and encourage them to point to the appropriate answer to the question you are asking.

Other coloured boxes in the book – this time without the symbol –– give alphabetical listings of themed words with their English translations beside them.

For extra clarity, we have put all English words and phrases in black, foreign language terms in red and their phonetic pronunciation in italic.

This phrase book covers all subjects you are likely to come across during the course of your visit, from reserving a room for the night to ordering food and drink at a restaurant and what to do if your car breaks down or you lose your traveller's cheques and money. With over 2,000 commonly used words and essential phrases at your fingertips you can rest assured that you will be able to get by in all situations, so let the essential Phrase Book become your passport to a secure and enjoyable trip!

Pronunciation table

The pronunciation provided should be read as if it were English, bearing in mind the following main points:

Vowels

a, **e**, **i**, and **o** are pronounced very much as they are in English. Please note that a capital I has a dot over the top like this: **İ**. A capital **I** without a dot is the upper case form of ı (see below).

u is almost exactly like the English sound **oo**.

ı is pronounced rather like the English sound **er** as in 'letter', or the sound **uh**. In the transcriptions it is given as **uh**.

ü is given as **ew**.

ö is transcribed here as **ur**, with a small **r**. *Do not confuse this with the slightly rolled consonant r (shown as **R** in the middle and at the end of words).*

Vowel blends **ai** and **ay** are pronounced like **i** as in 'side'. The symbol **í** is used to represent this sound.

As mentioned above, hyphens have been used to separate double consonants (which are pronounced separately). In other places, hyphens are also used to separate strings of letters which might otherwise be misread (eg **adaya** is read as **ada-ya**, not **aday-a**).

Consonants

The Turkish **ğ** (soft g) is not pronounced, but it slightly lengthens the preceding vowel; it is represented as a colon(:).

Mostly, **h** is pronounced as in English, but in some words, there is a different, slightly guttural h sound. This is shown as **H**.

The Turkish **r** is slightly rolled, *and always audibly pronounced*. As a reminder that it should be pronounced every time, when it occurs in the middle or at the end of a word, it is written as **R**.

ç is like the English **ch**.

Ş is the same as **sh** in English.
j is given as **zh**.

Double consonants in Turkish (as in **dükkan**) take twice as long to say as single consonants. The effect is a little like saying them twice. In the transliterated phrases, words with double consonants have been hyphenated as a reminder (eg **res-sam**).

Stress

Turkish words are mostly very lightly stressed – usually on the last syllable. The commonest exception comes with verbs containing the negative *mi* suffix in them, where the stress is thrown back onto the syllable before the **mi**.

Place names have the stress on the first syllable (except for Antalya and Istanbul, where it is on the middle syllable). However, some foreign loan-words (Arabic and Persian) do not conform to Turkish rules at all, and here the stress is shown with bold lettering.

1 Useful lists

1.1 Today or tomorrow?

What day is it today? ____	**Bugün günlerden ne?**
	boogewn gewnleRden neh?
Today's Monday _____	**Bugün günlerden pazartesi**
	boogewn gewnleRden pazaRtesi
– Tuesday _____	**Bugün günlerden salı**
	boogewn gewnleRden saluh
– Wednesday _____	**Bugün günlerden çarşamba**
	boogewn gewnleRden chaRshamba
– Thursday _____	**Bugün günlerden perşembe**
	boogewn gewnleRden peRshembeh
– Friday _____	**Bugün günlerden cuma**
	boogewn gewnleRden jooma
– Saturday _____	**Bugün günlerden cumartesi**
	boogewn gewnleRden joomaRtesi
– Sunday_____	**Bugün günlerden pazar**
	boogewn gewnleRden pazaR
in January_____	**ocakta**
	ojakta
since February _____	**şubattan beri**
	shoobat-tan beRi
in spring _____	**ilkbaharda**
	ilkba-haRda
in summer_____	**yazın/yazları**
	yazuhn/yazlaRuh
in autumn _____	**sonbaharda**
	sonba-haRda
in winter _____	**kışın/kışları**
	kuhshuhn/kuhshlaRuh
1997 _____	**bin dokuz yüz doksan yedi**
	bin dokooz yewz doksan yedi
the twentieth century ____	**XX. (yirminci) yüzyıl**
	yiRminji yewzyuhl
What's the date today? __	**Bugün ayın kaçı?**
	boogewn ayuhn kachuh?

Today's the 24th _____	**Bugün ayın 24'ü**
	boogewn ayuhn yiRmi durRdewnjew
Monday 3 November ____ 1998	**Pazartesi, 3 Kasım 1998**
	pazaRtesi, ewch kasuhm 1998
in the morning _____	**sabahleyin**
	sabaHleyin
in the afternoon_____	**öğleden sonra**
	urleden sonRa
in the evening _____	**akşamleyin**
	akshamleyin
at night _____	**geceleyin**
	gejeleyin
this morning_____	**bu sabah**
	boo sabaH
this afternoon_____	**bugün öğleden sonra**
	boogewn ur:leden sonRa
this evening _____	**bu akşam**
	boo aksham
tonight_____	**bu gece**
	boo gejeh
last night_____	**dün gece**
	dewn gejeh
this week _____	**bu hafta**
	boo hafta
next month_____	**gelecek ay**
	gelejek í
last year _____	**geçen sene**
	gechen seneh
next... _____	**gelecek...**
	gelejek...
in...days/weeks/ _____ months/years	**...gün/hafta/ay/sene sonra**
	...gewn/hafta/i/seneh sonRa
...weeks ago_____	**...hafta önce**
	...hafta urnjeh
day off_____	**tatil günü**
	tatil gewnewĕ

1.2 Bank holidays

● **Public** holidays and **religious** observance:
Public holidays

1 January	Yılbaşı (New Year)
23 April	Ulusal Egemenlik ve Çocuk Bayramı (National Sovereignty and Children's Day)
19 May	Gençlik ve Spor Bayramı (Young People's and Sports Day)
30 August	Zafer Bayramı (Victory Day)
29 October	Cumhuriyet Bayramı (Republic Day)

Major Religious Festivals

The *Şeker Bayramı* (the Feast of Breaking Fast) is a three-day festival marking the end of Ramadan. Its date each year varies with the timing of Ramadan. Information on the precise date should be readily available before you travel.

The *Kurban Bayramı* (the Feast of Sacrifice) follows two months later, and is a four-day celebration which traditionally has been associated with the sacrifice of a ram.

Shops, banks and offices are closed on all these days.

If at any time you should wish to enter a mosque during your visit, be ready to remove your shoes at the entrance. Women should also cover their heads (a headscarf can often be borrowed from the mosque itself). Both shorts and short skirts are inappropriate.

You should also without fail remove your shoes before entering a private house.

1.3 What time is it?

What time is it?	_____	**Saat kaç?** *saht kach?*
It's nine o'clock	_____	**Saat dokuz** *saht dokooz*

– five past ten _____	**Saat onu beş geçiyor**	
	saht onoo besh gechiyoR	
– a quarter past eleven __	**Saat on biri çeyrek geçiyor**	
	saht on biRi cheyrek gechiyoR	
– twenty past twelve_____	**Saat on ikiyi yirmi geçiyor**	
	saht on ikiyi yiRmi gechiyoR	
– half past one_____	**Saat bir buçuk**	
	saht biR boochook	
– twenty–five to three____	**Saat üçe yirmi beş var**	
	saht ewcheh yiRmi besh vaR	
– a quarter to four_____	**Saat dörde çeyrek var**	
	saht durRdeh cheyRek vaR	
– ten to five _____	**Saat beşe on var**	
	saht besheh on vaR	
– twelve noon _____	**Öğlen saat on iki**	
	ur:len saht on iki	
– midnight_____	**Gece on iki**	
	gejeh on iki	
half an hour _____	**yarım saat**	
	yaRuhm saht	
What time?_____	**Saat kaçta?**	
	saht kachta?	
What time can I come ___ round?	**Saat kaçta uğrayayım?**	
	saht kachta u:Ra-ya-yuhm?	
At... _____	**Saat...de**	
	saht...deh	
After... _____	**den...sonra**	
	den...sonRa	
Before... _____	**den...önce**	
	den...urnjeh	
Between...and... _____	**...le...arası**	
	...ileh...aRasuh	
From...to... _____	**...den...kadar**	
	...den...kadaR	
In...minutes_____	**...dakika sonra**	
	...dakika sonRa	

– an hour _____	...saat sonra	
		...saht sonRa
– a quarter of an hour ___	On beş dakika sonra	
		on besh dakika sonRa
– three quarters of _____	Kırk beş dakika sonra	
an hour		*kuhRk besh dakika sonRa*
early/late _____	çok erken/geç	
		chok eRken/gech
on time _____	zamanında	
		zamanuhnda
summertime _____	yaz mevsimi	
		yaz mevsimi
wintertime _____	kış mevsimi	
		kuhsh mevsimi

1.4 One, two, three...

0 _____	sıfır	*suhfuhR*
1 _____	bir	*biR*
2 _____	iki	*iki*
3 _____	üç	*ewch*
4 _____	dört	*durRt*
5 _____	beş	*besh*
6 _____	altı	*altuh*
7 _____	yedi	*yedi*
8 _____	sekiz	*sekiz*
9 _____	dokuz	*dokooz*
10 _____	on	*on*
11 _____	on bir	*on biR*
12 _____	on iki	*on iki*
13 _____	on üç	*on ewch*
14 _____	on dört	*on durRt*
15 _____	on beş	*on besh*
16 _____	on altı	*on altuh*
17 _____	on yedi	*on yedi*

18	_____	on sekiz	*on sekiz*
19	_____	on dokuz	*on dokooz*
20	_____	yirmi	*yiRmi*
21	_____	yirmi bir	*yiRmi biR*
22	_____	yirmi iki	*yiRmi iki*
30	_____	otuz	*otooz*
31	_____	otuz bir	*otooz biR*
32	_____	otuz iki	*otooz iki*
40	_____	kırk	*kuhRk*
50	_____	elli	*el-li*
60	_____	altmış	*altmuhsh*
70	_____	yetmiş	*yetmish*
80	_____	seksen	*seksen*
90	_____	doksan	*oksan*
100	_____	yüz	*yewz*
101	_____	yüz bir	*yewz biR*
110	_____	yüz on	*yewz on*
120	_____	yüz yirmi	*yewz yiRmi*
200	_____	iki yüz	*iki yewz*
300	_____	üç yüz	*ewch yewz*
400	_____	dört yüz	*durRt yewz*
500	_____	beş yüz	*besh yewz*
600	_____	altı yüz	*altuh yewz*
700	_____	yedi yüz	*yedi yewz*
800	_____	sekiz yüz	*sekiz yewz*
900	_____	dokuz yüz	*dokooz yewz*
1000	_____	bin	*bin*
1100	_____	bin yüz	*bin yewz*
2000	_____	iki bin	*iki bin*
10,000	_____	on bin	*on bin*
100,000	_____	yüz bin	*yewz bin*
1,000,000	_____	milyon	*mil-yon*
1st	_____	birinci	*biRinji*
2nd	_____	ikinci	*ikinji*
3rd	_____	üçüncü	*ewchewnjew*
4th	_____	dördüncü	*durRdewnjew*

5th _____	**beşinci**	*beshinji*
6th _____	**altıncı**	*altuhnjuh*
7th _____	**yedinci**	*yedinji*
8th _____	**sekizinci**	*sekizinji*
9th _____	**dokuzuncu**	*dokoozoonjoo*
10th _____	**onuncu**	*onoonjoo*
11th _____	**on birinci**	*on biRinji*
12th _____	**on ikinci**	*on ikinji*
13th _____	**on üçüncü**	*on ewchewnjew*
14th _____	**on dördüncü**	*on durRdewnjew*
15th _____	**on beşinci**	*on beshinji*
16th _____	**on altıncı**	*on altuhnjuh*
17th _____	**on yedinci**	*on yedinji*
18th _____	**on sekizinci**	*on sekizinji*
19th _____	**on dokuzuncu**	*on dokoozoonjoo*
20th _____	**yirminci**	*yiRminji*
21st _____	**yirmi birinci**	*yiRmi biRinji*
22nd _____	**yirmi ikinci**	*yiRmi ikinji*
30th _____	**otuzuncu**	*otoozoonjoo*
100th _____	**yüzüncü**	*yewzewnjew*
1000th _____	**bininci**	*bininji*

once _____	**bir kere**	
	biR keReh	
twice _____	**iki kere**	
	iki keReh	
double _____	**iki katı**	
	iki katuh	
triple _____	**üç katı**	
	ewch katuh	
half _____	**yarısı**	
	yaRuhsuh	
a quarter _____	**dörtte biri**	
	durRt-teh biRi	
a third _____	**üçte biri**	
	ewchteh biRi	

16

a couple, a few, some ___	**bir çift, birkaç, bazı**
	biR chift, biRkach, bazuh
2+4=6 _____	**iki artı dört eşittir altı**
	iki aRtuh durRt eshit-tiR altuh
4-2=2_____	**dört eksi iki eşittir iki**
	durRt eksi iki eshit-tiR iki
2x4=8 _____	**iki çarpı dört eşittir sekiz**
	iki chaRpuh durRt eshit-tiR sekiz
4÷2=2 _____	**dört bölü iki eşittir iki**
	durRt burlew iki eshit-tiR iki
odd/even _____	**tek/çift**
	tek/chift
total _____	**toplam**
	toplam
6x9_____	**altı çarpı dokuz**
	altuh chaRpuh dokooz

1.5 The weather

Is the weather going____ to be good/bad?	**Hava güzel mi/kötü mü olacak?**
	hava gewzel mi/kurtew mew olajak?
Is it going to get _____ colder/hotter?	**Hava soğuk mu/sıcak mı olacak?**
	hava so:ook moo/suhjak muh olajak?
What temperature is it ___ going to be?	**Hava kaç derece olacak?**
	hava kach deRejeh olajak?
Is it going to rain?_____	**Yağmur mu yağacak?**
	ya:mooR moo ya:ajak?
Is there going to be a____ storm?	**Hava fırtınalı mı olacak?**
	hava fuhRtuhnaluh muh olajak?
Is it going to snow? ____	**Kar mı yağacak?**
	kahR muh ya:ajak?
Is it going to freeze?____	**Don mu olacak?**
	don moo olajak?

17

Is the thaw setting in? ___ **Buzlar mı eriyecek?**
boozlaR muh eRiyejek?

Is it going to be foggy? __ **Hava sisli mi olacak?**
hava sisli mi olajak?

Is there going to be a ___ **Fırtına mı çıkacak?**
thunderstorm? *fuhRtuhna muh chuhkajak?*

The weather's _____ **Hava değişiyor**
changing *hava de:ishiyoR*

It's cooling down_____ **Hava soğuyor**
hava so:ooyor

What's the weather_____ **Bugün/yarın hava nasıl olacak?**
going to be like today/ *Boogewn/yaruhn hava nasuhl olajak?*
tomorrow?

aniden şiddetlenen rüzgar	**güneşli**	**sağanak yağış**
sudden squall	sunny	heavy downpour
az bulutlu	**güzel**	**serin**
almost cloudless	beautiful	cool
boğucu sıcaklık	**hafif/şiddetli rüzgar**	**sıcak**
stifling heat	light/strong wind	hot
bulut	**ılımlı**	**sıcak hava dalgası**
cloud	moderate	heat wave
bunaltıcı	**kar**	**(sıfırın altında/üstünde)**
oppressive	snow	**...derece**
çok bulutlu	**kasırga**	...degrees
very cloudy	cyclone, hurricane	below/above zero
dolu	**kırağı**	**sis**
hail	hoar frost	fog
don	**parçalı bulutlu**	**yağmur**
ice	with patchy cloud	rain
fırtına	**rüzgar**	**yağmurlu**
storm	wind	rainy
fırtınalı	**rüzgarlı**	
stormy	windy	

1.6 Here, there...

See also 5.1 Asking for directions

here/there _____	**burada/orada**
	booRada/oRada
somewhere/nowhere _____	**herhangi bir yerde/hiç bir yerde**
	heRhangi biR yeRdeh/hich biR yeRdeh
everywhere _____	**her yerde**
	heR yeRdeh
far away/nearby _____	**uzak/yakın**
	oozak/yakuhn
right/left _____	**sağ/sol**
	sa:/sol
to the right/left of _____	**sağında/solunda**
	sa:uhnda/soloonda
straight ahead _____	**doğru**
	do:Roo
via _____	**...yoluyla**
	...yolooyla
in _____	**...içine/içinde**
	...ichineh/ichindeh
on _____	**...üzerine/üzerinde**
	...ewzeRineh/ewzeRindeh
under _____	**...altına/altında**
	...altuhna/altuhnda
against _____	**...karşı**
	...kaRshuh
opposite _____	**karşısında**
	kaRshuhsuhnda
next to _____	**...yanında**
	...yanuhnda
near _____	**...yakın**
	...yakuhn
in front of _____	**...önünde**
	...urnewndeh

in the centre	_____	**ortada**
		oRtada
forward	_____	**öne**
		urneh
down	_____	**aşağı (aşağıya)**
		asha:uh (asha:uh-ya)
up	_____	**yukarı (yukarıya)**
		yookaRuh (yookaRuh-ya)
inside	_____	**içeri (içeriye)**
		icheRi (icheRiyeh)
outside	_____	**dışarı (dışarıya)**
		duhshaRuh (duhshaRuh-ya)
behind	_____	**arka (arkaya)**
		aRka (aRka-ya)
at the front	_____	**ön tarafta**
		urn taRafta
at the back	_____	**arka tarafta**
		aRka taRafta
in the north	_____	**kuzeyde**
		koozeydeh
to the south	_____	**güneye**
		gewneyeh
from the west	_____	**batıdan**
		batuhdan
from the east	_____	**doğudan**
		do:oodan
...of	_____	**...de/da**
		...-deh/-da

1.7 What does that sign say?

See also 5.4 Traffic signs

açık/kapalı
open/closed
acil çıkış
emergency exit
açılış saatleri
opening hours
asansör lift
ateş yakmak yasaktır
no open fires
bayanlar tuvaleti
ladies toilet
bozuk
out of order
çay bahçesi
tea garden
çıkış
way out
**danışma,
enformasyon**
information
dikkat
take care, beware
dikkat köpek var
beware of the dog
dolu
full
durak
(bus) stop
emanet
left luggage
erkekler tuvaleti
gentlemen's toilet

**fotoğraf çekmek
yasaktır**
no photographs
giriş
entrance
girmek yasaktır
no entry, no
admittance
gişe, vezne
pay here
istasyon
station
itiniz/çekiniz
push/pull
kalkış
departure
kamping
camping, camp-site
karakol
police station
kasa
pay here
...kat
...floor
kiralık
for hire
merdiven
stairs
merkez
centre
otel
hotel

pansiyon
bed and breakfast
pasaj arcade
peron
platform
PTT PTT (main post
office and public
telephones)
resepsiyon
reception
satılık
for sale
seyahat acentası
travel agent
sigara içmek yasaktır
no smoking
tehlike
danger
tuvaletler
toilets
vestiyer
cloakroom
yangın merdiveni
fire escape
yangın tehlikesi
danger – fire
yerlere tükürmeyiniz
no spitting
yüksek voltaj
high voltage
yürüyen merdiven
escalator

1.8 Telephone alphabet

a	*ah*	**Adana**	*adana*
b	*beh*	**Bursa**	*booRsa*
c	*jeh*	**Cide**	*jideh*
ç	*cheh*	**Çanakkale**	*chanak- kaleh*
d	*deh*	**Denizli**	*denizli*
e	*eh*	**Edirne**	*ediRneh*
f	*feh*	**Fethiye**	*fet-hiyeh*
g	*geh*	**Giresun**	*giResoon*
ğ	*yoomooshak geh* (no Turkish words begin with ğ)		
h	*heh*	**Hatay**	*hatí*
i	*i*	**İzmir**	*izmiR*
ı	*uh*	**Isparta**	*uhspaRta*
j	*zheh*	**Japonya**	*zhaponya*
k	*keh*	**Konya**	*konya*
l	*leh*	**Lüleburgaz**	*lewlebooRgaz*
m	*meh*	**Malatya**	*malatya*
n	*neh*	**Nevşehir**	*nevshe-hiR*
o	*o*	**Ordu**	*oRdoo*
ö	*ur*	**Ören**	*urRen*
p	*peh*	**Pamukkale**	*pamook-kaleh*
r	*reh*	**Rize**	*rizeh*
s	*seh*	**Sinop**	*sinop*
ş	*sheh*	**Şirvan**	*shiRvan*
t	*teh*	**Tokat**	*tokat*
u	*oo*	**Urfa**	*ooRfa*
ü	*ew*	**Üsküp**	*ewskewp*
v	*veh*	**Van**	*van*
y	*yeh*	**Yozgat**	*yozgat*
z	*zeh*	**Zonguldak**	*zongooldak*

1.9 Personal details

surname _____	**soyadı**	
	soy-aduh	
forename(s) _____	**adı**	
	aduh	
initials _____	**ismin baş harfleri**	
	ismin bash haRfleRi	
address (street/number)__	**adres (sokak/numara)**	
	adRes (sokak/noomaRa)	
post code/town _____	**posta kodu/oturduğu yer**	
	posta kodoo/otooRdoo:oo yeR	
sex (male/female) _____	**cinsiyeti (erkek, kadın)**	
	jinsiyeti (eRkek/kaduhn)	
nationality _____	**uyruğu**	
	ooyRoo:oo	
date of birth _____	**doğum tarihi**	
	do:oom tahRi-hi	
place of birth _____	**doğum yeri**	
	do:oom yeRi	
occupation _____	**mesleği**	
	mesle:i	
married/single/divorced __	**evli/bekar/boşanmış**	
	evli/bekahR/boshanmuhsh	
widowed _____	**dul**	
	dool	
(number of) children _____	**çocukları (sayısı)**	
	chojooklaRuh (sa-yuhsuh)	
passport/identity _____	**pasaport/ehliyet numarası**	
card/driving licence	*pasapoRt/eHliyet noomaRasuh*	
number		
place and date of issue __	**verildiği tarih ve yer**	
	veRildi:i taRiH veh yeR	

2 Courtesies

● Greetings are very popular, everyone is asked individually if they're all right. When introduced people shake hands, when they part they also shake hands.
If they know each other people kiss on both cheeks (usually man to man, woman to woman).

2.1 Greetings

Hello, Mr John Smith ____	**Merhaba John Bey**
	meR-haba John Bey
Hello, Mrs Barbara Jones	**Merhaba Barbara Hanim**
	meR-haba, Barbara Hanuhm
Hello, Peter _____	**Merhaba, Peter**
	meR-haba, Peter
Hi, Helen_____	**Selam, Helen**
	selam, Helen
Good morning, madam __	**Günaydın hanımefendi**
	gewníduhn hanuhmefendi
Good afternoon, sir _____	**İyi günler beyefendi**
	iyi gewnleR bey-efendi
Good evening _____	**İyi akşamlar**
	iyi akshamlaR
How are you? _____	**Nasılsınız, iyi misiniz?**
	nasuhlsuhnuhz, iyi misiniz?
Fine, thank you,_____ and you?	**Teşekkür ederim. Siz nasılsınız?**
	teshek-kewR edeRim. siz nasuhlsuhnuhz?
Very well _____	**Çok iyiyim, teşekkür ederim**
	chok iyiyim, teshek-kewR edeRim
Not very well _____	**İyi değilim**
	iyi de:ilim
Not too bad _____	**İdare eder**
	idaReh edeR
I'd better be going _____	**Ben gideyim artık**
	ben gideyim aRtuhk
I have to be going_____	**Gitmek zorundayım. Beni bekliyorlar**
	gitmek zoRoonda-yim. beni bekli-yoRlaR

25

Someone's waiting _____ for me Bye!	**Görüşürüz!**
	gurRewshewRewz!
Goodbye_____	**Güle güle/Allaha ısmarladık**
	gewleh gewleh/al-laha uhsmaRladuhk
See you soon_____	**görüşmek üzere**
	gurRewshmek ewzeReh
See you later _____	**Sonra görüşmek üzere**
	sonRa gurRewshmek ewzeReh
See you in a little while __	**En kısa zamanda görüşmek üzere**
	en kuhsa zamanda gurRewshmek ewzeReh
Sleep well_____	**İyi uykular**
	iyi ooykoolaR
Good night _____	**İyi geceler**
	iyi gejeleR
All the best_____	**Sağlıcakla kalın**
	sa:luhjakla kaluhn
Have fun _____	**İyi eğlenceler**
	iyi e:lenjeleR
Good luck_____	**İyi şanslar**
	iyi shanslaR
Have a nice holiday _____	**İyi tatiller**
	iyi tatil-leR
Have a good trip _____	**İyi yolculuklar**
	iyi yoljoolooklaR
Thank you, you too_____	**Teşekkürler, size de**
	teshek-kewRleR, sizeh deh
Say hello to...for me _____	**e... selamlarımı söyleyin**
	selamlaRuhmuh suhy-leh-yin

2.2 How to ask a question

Who?_____	**Kim?**
	kim
Who's that? _____	**O kim?**
	o kim?

What? _____	**Ne?**
	neh?
What's there to _____ see here?	**Burada görülecek ne var?**
	booRada gurRewlejek neh vaR?
What kind of hotel_____ is that?	**O nasıl bir otel?**
	o nasuhl biR otel?
Where? _____	**Nerede?**
	neRedeh?
Where's the toilet? _____	**Tuvalet ne tarafta?**
	too-alet neh taRafta?
Where are you going? ___	**Nereye gidiyorsunuz?**
	neRe-yeh gidiyoRsoonooz?
Where are you from? ____	**Nerelisiniz?**
	neRelisiniz?
How?_____	**Nasıl?**
	nasuhl?
How far is that?_____	**Orası ne kadar uzak?**
	oRasuh neh kadaR oozak?
How long does that take?	**Ne kadar sürer?**
	neh kadaR sewReR?
How long is the trip? ___	**Yolculuk ne kadar sürer?**
	yoljoolook neh kadaR sewReR?
How much? _____	**Ne kadar?**
	neh kadaR?
How much is this? _____	**Bunun fiyatı ne kadar?**
	boonoon fi-yatuh neh kadaR?
What time is it? _____	**Saat kaç?**
	saht kach?
Which? _____	**Hangi? Hangileri?**
	hangi? hangileRi?
Which glass is mine? ____	**Hangi bardak benim?**
	hangi baRdak benim?
When?_____	**Ne zaman?**
	neh zaman?
When are you leaving?___	**Yola ne zaman çıkıyorsunuz?**
	yola neh zaman chuhkuh-yoRsoonooz?

Why? _____	**Niçin?** *nichin?*
Could you...me? _____	**Bana...?** *bana...?*
Could you help me, _____ please?	**Bana yardım edebilir misiniz?** *bana yaRduhm edebiliR misiniz?*
Could you point that_____ out to me?	**Onu bana gösterebilir misiniz?** *onoo bana gursteRebiliR misisniz?*
Could you come _____ with me, please?	**Benimle gelebilir misiniz?** *benimleh beRabeR gelebiliR misiniz?*
Could you... _____	**...-ir misiniz?/mısınız?** *...-iR misiniz?/muhsuhnuz?*
Could you reserve some _ tickets for me, please?	**Benim için birkaç bilet ayırır mısınız, lütfen?** *benim ichin biRkach bilet í-uhRuhR muhsuhnuhz?*
Do you know...? _____	**...biliyor musunuz?** *...biliyoR moosoonooz?*
Do you know another_____ hotel, please?	**Başka bir otel biliyor musunuz?** *bashka biR otel biliyoR moosoonooz?*
Do you have a...? _____	**...var mı?** *...vaR muh?*
Do you have a...for me? _	**Benim için...var mı?** *benim ichin...vaR muh?*
Do you have a _____ vegetarian dish, please?	**Etsiz bir yemeğiniz var mı?** *etsiz bir yeme:iniz vaR muh?*
I'd like... _____	**...istiyorum** *...istiyoRoom*
I'd like a kilo of apples, _ please	**Bir kilo elma istiyorum** *biR kilo elma istiyoRoom*
Can I...? _____	**abilir/ebilir miyim?** *-abiliR/-ebiliR miyim?*
Can I take this? _____	**Bunu alabilir miyim?** *boonoo alabiliR miyim?*
Can I smoke here? _____	**Burada sigara içebilir miyim?** *booRada sigaRa ichebiliR miyim?*
Could I ask you _____ something?	**Bir şey sorabilir miyim?** *BiR shey soRabiliR mi-yim?*

2.3 How to reply

Yes, of course _____	**Evet, tabii** *evet tabee*
No, I'm sorry _____	**Hayır, özür dilerim** *ha-yuhR urzewR dileRim*
Yes, what can I do _____ for you?	**Evet, size nasıl yardımcı olabilirim?** *evet, sizeh nasuhl yaRduhmjuh olabiliRim?*
Just a moment, please __	**Bir saniye lütfen** *biR sahniyeh lewtfen*
No, I don't have_____ time now	**Hayır, şu anda hiç zamanım yok** *ha-yiR shoo anda hich zamanuhm yok*
No, that's impossible ____	**Hayır, imkansız** *ha-yuhR imkahnsuhz*
I think so_____	**Zannederim** *zan-nedeRim*
I agree_____	**Bence de** *benjeh deh*
I hope so too _____	**Umarım** *oomaRuhm*
No, not at all _____	**Hayır** *ha-yuhR*
No, no-one_____	**Hayır, hiç kimse** *ha-yuhR hich kimseh*
No, nothing _____	**Hayır, hiç bir şey** *ha-yuhR hich biR shey*
That's (not) right _____	**Doğru (doğru değil)** *do:Roo (do:Roo de:il)*
I (don't) agree_____	**Sizinle aynı fikirdeyim (fikirde değilim)** *sizinleh ínuh fikiRdeyim (fikiRdeh de:ilim)*
All right _____	**İyi** *iyi*
Okay _____	**Tamam** *tamam*
Perhaps_____	**Belki** *belki*
I don't know_____	**Bilmiyorum** *bilmiyoRoom*

2.4 Thank you

Thank you	**Teşekkür ederim** *teshek-kewR edeRim*
You're welcome	**Bir şey değil** *biR shey de:il*
Thank you very much	**Çok teşekkür ederim** *chok teshek-kewR edeRim*
Very kind of you	**Çok naziksiniz** *chok naziksiniz*
I enjoyed it very much	**Benim için büyük bir zevkti** *benim ichin bew-yewk biR zevkti*
Thank you for your trouble	**Zahmet ettiniz, teşekkür ederim** *zaHmet et-tiniz, teshek-kewR edeRim*
You shouldn't have	**Bunu yapmamalıydınız** *boonoo yapmamaluhy-duhnuhz*
That's all right	**Hiç önemli değil** *hich urnemli de:il*

2.5 Sorry

Sorry!	**Pardon!** *paRdon!*
Excuse me	**Özür dilerim** *urzewR dileRim*
I'm sorry, I didn't know...	**Özür dilerim, ... bilmiyordum** *urzewR dileRim ... bilmiyoRdoom*
I do apologise	**Affedersiniz** *af-fedeRsiniz*
I'm sorry	**Çok üzgünüm** *chok ewzgewnewm*
I didn't do it on purpose, it was an accident	**Kasten yapmadım, yanlışlıkla oldu** *kasten yapmaduhm, yanluhshluhkla oldoo*

That's all right	**Önemli değil**
	urnemli de:il
Never mind	**Boş ver**
	bosh veR
It could've happened to_	**Herkesin başına gelebilir**
anyone	*heRkesin bashuhna gelebiliR*

2.6 What do you think?

Which do you prefer?___	**Neyi tercih edersiniz?**
	neyi teRji-hedeRsiniz?
What do you think? ____	**Ne dersiniz?**
	neh deRsiniz?
Don't you like dancing? _	**Dans etmeyi sevmiyor musun?**
	dans etmeyi sevmiyoR moosoon?
I don't mind	**Benim için fark etmez**
	benim ichin faRk etmez
Well done!	**Bravo!**
	bRavo!
Not bad!	**Fena değil!**
	fena de:il!
Great!	**Şahane!**
	sha-haneh!
Wonderful!	**Harika!**
	haRika!
It's really nice here!	**Burası ne eğlenceli!**
	booRasuh neh e:lenjili!
How nice!	**Ne hoş/güzel!**
	neh hosh/gewzel!
How nice for you!	**Sizin için ne iyi!**
	sizin ichin neh iyi!
I'm (not) very happy	**...çok memnunum (memnun değilim)**
with...	*...chok memnoonoom (memnoon de:ilim)*
I'm glad...	**...memnun oldum**
	...memnoon oldoom

I'm having a great time __	**Çok eğleniyorum**
	chok e:leniyoroom
I'm looking forward to it__	**Sabırsızlıkla bekliyorum**
	sabuhRsuhzluhkla bekliyoRoom
I hope it'll work out_____	**Umarım olur**
	oomaRuhm oloor
That's ridiculous!_____	**Ne gülünç!**
	neh gewlewnch!
That's terrible! _____	**Ne iğrenç!**
	neh i:Rench!
What a pity! _____	**Ne yazık!**
	neh yazuhk!
That's filthy! _____	**Ne pis!**
	ne pis!
What a load of rubbish! __	**Ne saçmalık!**
	neh sachmaluhk!
I don't like... _____	**...sevmiyorum**
	...sevmiyoRoom
I'm bored to death _____	**Canım çok sıkılıyor**
	januhm chok suhkuhluhyoR
I've had enough _____	**Bıktım**
	buhktuhm
This is no good _____	**Bu böyle olmaz**
	boo buhyleh olmaz
I was expecting_____ something completely different	**Tamamen başka bir şey bekliyordum** *tamahmen bashka biR shey bekliyoRdoom*

3 Conversation

3.1 I beg your pardon?

I don't speak any/_____ I speak a little...	...**konuşmasını bilmiyorum/...biraz biliyorum** *...konooshmasuhnuh bilmiyoRoom/...biRaz biliyoRoom*
I'm English _____	**Ben İngilizim** *ben ingilizim*
I'm Scottish _____	**Ben İskoçyalıyım** *ben iskochyaluh-yuhm*
I'm Irish _____	**Ben İrlandalıyım** *ben iRlandaluh-yuhm*
I'm Welsh _____	**Ben Gallerliyim** *ben gal-leRliyim*
Do you speak_____ English/French/German?	**İngilizce/Fransızca/Almanca konuşmasını biliyor musunuz?** *ingilizje/fransuhzja/almanja konooshmasuhnuh biliyoR moosoonooz?*
Is there anyone who _____ speaks...?	...**konuşmasını bilen kimse var mı?** *...konushmasuhnuh bilen kimseh var muh?*
I beg your pardon? _____	**Ne dediniz?** *neh dediniz?*
I (don't) understand _____	**Sizi anlıyorum (anlamıyorum)** *sizi anluhyoRoom (anlamuhyoRoom)*
Do you understand me? _	**Beni anlıyor musunuz?** *beni anluhyoR moosoonooz?*
Could you repeat that, ___ please?	**Lütfen tekrar eder misiniz?** *lewtfen tekRaR edeR misiniz?*
Could you speak more___ slowly, please?	**Biraz daha yavaş konuşabilir misiniz?** *biRaz da-ha yavash konooshabiliR misiniz?*
What does that (word) ___ mean?	**O/o sözcük ne demek?** *o/o surzjewk neh demek?*
Is that similar to/the _____ same as...?	...**(hemen hemen) aynısı mı?** *...(hemen hemen) ínuhsuh muh?*

Could you write that _____ **Onu benim için bir kağıda yazabilir**
down for me, please?   **misiniz?**

onoo benim ichin biR ka:uhda yazabiliR
misiniz?

Could you spell that _____ **Onu benim için heceleyebilir misiniz?**
for me, please?   *onoo benim ichin hejeleyebiliR misiniz?*

(See 1.8 Telephone alphabet)

Could you point that _____ **Onu bana bu rehberde gösterebilir misiniz?**
out in this phrase book,   *onoo bana boo reHbeRdeh gursteRebiliR*
please?   *misiniz?*

One moment, please, _____   **Bir saniye, sözcüğü aramam gerek**
I have to look it up   *biR sahniyeh, surzjew:ew aRamam geRek*

I can't find the word/the _ **Sözcüğü/cümleyi bulamıyorum**
sentence   *surzjew:ew/jewmleyi boolamuhyoRoom*

How do you say _____   **...ona ne diyorsunuz?**
that in...?   *...ona neh diyoRsoonooz?*

How do you pronounce __   **Onu nasıl telaffuz ediyorsunuz?**
that?   *onoo nasuhl telaf-fooz ediyoRsoonooz*

3.2 Introductions

May I introduce myself? _   **Kendimi tanıtabilir miyim?**
                            kendimi tanuhtabiliR miyim?

My name's..._____   **Benim adım...**
                            benim aduhm..

I'm... _____   **Ben...**
                            ben...

What's your name?_____   **Adınız ne?**
                            aduhnuhz neh?

May I introduce...? _____   **Size...tanıtabilir miyim?**
                            size...tanuhtabiliR miyim?

This is my wife/ _____ daughter/mother/ girlfriend	**Bu benim eşim/kızım/annem/kız arkadaşım.** *boo benim eshim/kuhzuhm/an-nem/kuhz aRkadashuhm*
– my husband/son/_____ father/boyfriend	**Bu benim eşim/oğlum/babam/erkek arkadaşım.** *boo benim eshim/o:loom/babam/eRkek aRkadashuhm*
How do you do _____	**Memnum oldum** *memnoom oldoom*
Pleased to meet you ____	**(Tanıştığımıza) memnun oldum** *(tanuhshtuh:uhmuhza) memnoon oldoom*
Where are you from? ____	**Nerelisiniz?** *neRelisiniz?*
I'm from _____ England/Scotland/ Ireland/Wales	**Ben İngilizim/İSkoçyalıyım/İrlandalıyım/ Gallerliyim** *ben ingilizim/iskochyaluh-yuhm/iRlandaluh-yuhm/gal-leRliyim*
What city do you live in? _	**Hangi şehirde oturuyorsunuz?** *hangi she-hiRdeh otooRooyoRsoonooz?*
In..., It's near... _____	**..., ...yakın** *..., ...yakuhn*
Have you been here _____ long?	**Uzun zamandan beri mi buradasınız?** *oozoon zamandan beRi mi booRadasuhnuhz?*
A few days _____	**Birkaç günden beri buradayım** *biRkach gewnden beRi booRada-yuhm*
How long are you _____ staying here?	**Burada ne kadar kalacaksınız?** *booRada neh kadaR kalajaksuhnuhz?*
We're (probably) leaving _ tomorrow/in two weeks	**(Büyük bir olasılıkla) yarın/iki hafta sonra yola çıkacağız** *bewyewk biR olasuhluhkla yaRuhn/iki hafta sonRa yola chuhkaja:uhz*
Where are you staying? __	**Nerede kalıyorsunuz?** *neRedeh kaluhyoRsoonooz?*
In a hotel/an apartment __	**Bir otelde/apartman dairesinde** *biR oteldeh/apaRtaman díResindeh*

On a camp site _____	**Bir kampingde**	
	biR kampingdeh	
With friends/relatives ____	**Bir arkadaşın/ailenin yanında**	
	biR aRkadashuhn/ilenin yanuhnda	
Are you here on your ____ own/with your family?	**Burada yalnız mısınız/ailenizle misiniz?**	
	booRada yalnuhz muhsuhnuhz/ilenizleh misiniz?	
I'm on my own_____	**Yalnızım**	
	yalnuhzuhm	
I'm with my_____ partner/wife/husband	**Eşimleyim**	
	eshimleyim	
– with my family _____	**Ailemleyim**	
	ilemleyim	
– with relatives_____	**Akrabalarlayım**	
	akRabalaRla-yuhm	
– with a _____ boyfriend/girlfriend/ friends	**Erkek arkadaşımlayım/kız arkadaşımlayım/arkadaşlarımlayım**	
	eRkek aRkadashuhmla-yuhm/kuhz aRkadashuhmla-yuhm/ aRkadashlaRuhmla-yuhm	
Are you married?_____	**Evli misiniz?**	
	evli misiniz?	
Do you have a steady ____ boyfriend/girlfriend?	**Erkek/kız arkadaşın var mı?**	
	eRkek/kuhz aRkadashuhn vaR muh?	
That's none of your_____ business	**Sizi ilgilendirmez**	
	sizi ilgilendiRmez	
I'm married_____	**Evliyim**	
	evliyim	
– single _____	**Bekarım**	
	*bek**ahR**uhm*	
– separated _____	**Eşimden ayrı yaşıyorum**	
	eshimden íruh yashuhyoRoom	
– divorced_____	**Boşandım**	
	boshanduhm	
– a widow/widower_____	**Dulum**	
	dooloom	

I live alone/with _____ someone	**Yalnız/biriyle beraber yaşıyorum** *yalnuhz/biRiyleh beRabeR yashuhyoRoom*
Do you have any _____ children/grandchildren?	**Çocuklarınız/torunlarınız var mı?** *chojooklaRuhnuhz/toRoonlaRuhnuhz vaR muh?*
How old are you? _____	**Kaç yaşındasınız?** *kach yashuhndasuhnuhz?*
How old is she/he?_____	**O kaç yaşında?** *o kach yashuhnda?*
I'm... _____	**...yaşındayım** *...yashuhnda-yuhm*
She's/he's... _____	**O...yaşında** *o...yashuhnda*
What do you do for a ____ living?	**Ne iş yaparsınız?** *neh ish yapaRsuhnuhz?*
I work in an office _____	**Bir büroda çalışıyorum** *biR bewRoda chaluhshuhyoRoom*
I'm a student/ _____ I'm at school	**Okuyorum** *okooyoRoom*
I'm unemployed_____	**İşsizim** *ishsizim*
I'm retired _____	**Emekliyim** *emekliyim*
I'm on a disability _____ pension	**İş görmezlik sigortasından para alıyorum** *ish gurRmezlik sigoRtasuhndan paRa aluhyoRoom*
I'm a housewife_____	**Ev kadınıyım** *ev kaduhnuh-yuhm*
Do you like your job? ____	**İşinizi seviyor musunuz?** *ishinizi seviyoR moosoonooz?*
Most of the time _____	**Çoğu zaman** *cho:oo zaman*
I usually do, but I prefer__ holidays	**Genellikle seviyorum, ama tatil daha eğlenceli** *genel-likleh seviyoRoom ama tatil da-ha e:lenjeli*

3.3 Starting/ending a conversation

Could I ask you _____ something?	**Size bir şey sorabilir miyim?** *sizeh biR shey soRabiliR miyim?*
Excuse me _____	**Özür dilerim** *urzewR dileRim*
Excuse me, could you ___ help me?	**Özür dilerim, bana yardım edebilir misiniz?** *urzewR dileRim, bana yaRduhm edebiliR misiniz?*
Yes, what's the problem?	**Evet, sorun ne?** *evet, soRun neh?*
What can I do for you? __	**Size ne şekilde yardımcı olabilirim?** *sizeh neh shekildeh yaRduhmjuh olabiliRim?*
Sorry, I don't have time ___ now	**Kusura bakmayın, şu anda hiç zamanım yok** *koosooRa bakma-yuhn, shoo anda hich zamanuhm yok*
Do you have a light? ____	**Ateşiniz var mı?** *ateshiniz vaR muh?*
May I join you? _____	**Yanınıza oturabilir miyim?** *yanuhnuhza otooRabiliR miyim?*
Could you take a_____ picture of me/us? Press this button	**Resmimi/resmimizi çeker misiniz? Bu düğmeye basın** *resmimi/resmimizi chekeR misiniz? bu dew:meyeh basuhn*
Leave me alone_____	**Beni rahat bırak** *beni rahat buhRak*
Get lost _____	**Çekil git** *chekil git*
Go away or I'll scream ___	**Gitmezseniz, bağırırım** *gitmezseniz ba:uhRuhRuhm*

3.4 Congratulations and condolences

Happy birthday/many____
happy returns
Doğum gününüz kutlu olsun
do:oom gewnewnewz kootloo olsoon

Please accept my _____
condolences
Başınız sağ olsun
bashuhnuhz sa: olsoon

I'm very sorry for you ____
Sizin için çok üzgünüm
sizin ichin chok ewzgewnewm

3.5 A chat about the weather

See also 1.5 The weather

It's so hot/cold today! ___
Bugün hava ne kadar sıcak/soğuk!
boogewn hava neh kadaR suhjak/so:ook

Nice weather, isn't it?____
Hava güzel, değil mi?
hava gewzel, de:il mi?

What a wind/storm! _____
Bu ne rüzgar/fırtına!
boo neh rewzgaR/fuhRtuhna!

All that rain/snow! _____
Bu ne yağmur/kar!
boo neh ya:mooR/kahR!

All that fog!_____
Bu ne sis!
boo neh sis!

Has the weather been ___
like this for long here?
Hava uzun zamandan beri mi böyle?
hava oozoon zamandan beRi mi buhyleh?

Is it always this hot/cold _
here?
**Burası her zaman mı bu kadar
sıcak/soğuk?**
*booRasuh heR zaman muh boo kadaR
suhjak/so:ook?*

Is it always this dry/wet __
here?
**Burası her zaman mı bu kadar
kurak/yağışlı?**
*booRasuh heR zaman muh boo kadaR
kooRak/ya:uhshluh?*

3.6 Hobbies

Do you have any _____ hobbies?	**Boş zamanlarınızı nasıl değerlendirirsiniz?** *bosh zamanlaRuhnuhz nasuhl de:eRlendiRiRsiniz?*
I like painting/ _____ reading/photography/ DIY	**Resim yapmayı/kitap okumayı/fotoğraf çekmeyi/ufak tefek tamir işleri ile uğraşmayı severim** *urRgew urRmeyi/kitap okooma-yuh/foto:Raf chekmeyi/ufak tefek tahmir ishleRi ileh oo:Rashma-yuh seveRim*
I like music _____	**Müzik dinlemeyi severim** *mewzik dinlemeyi seveRim*
I like playing the _____ guitar/piano	**Gitar/piyano çalmayı severim** *gitaR/piyano chalma-yuh seveRim*
I like going to the movies	**Sinemaya gitmeyi severim** *sinema-ya gitmeyi seveRim*
I like travelling/ _____ sport/fishing/walking	**Seyahat etmeyi/spor yapmayı/balık tutmayı/yürümeyi severim** *seyahat etmeyi/spoR yapma-yuh/baluhk tootma-yuh/yewRewmeyi seveRim*

3.7 Being the host(ess)

See also 4 Eating out

Can I offer you a drink? __	**Size içecek bir şey ikram edebilir miyim?** *sizeh ichejek biR shey ikRahm edebiliR miyim?*
What would you like _____ to drink?	**Ne içersiniz?** *neh icheRsiniz?*
Something non-alcoholic, please	**Alkolsüz bir şey, lütfen** *alkolsewz biR shey, lewtfen*

| Would you like a _____ cigarette/cigar/to roll your own? | **Sigara/puro/sarma sigara içer misiniz?** *sigaRa/pooRo/saRma sigaRa icheR misiniz?* |
| I don't smoke _____ | **Sigara kullanmam** *sigaRa kul-lanmam* |

3.8 Invitations

Are you doing anything ___ tonight?	**Bu akşam meşgul müsünüz?** *boo aksham meshgool mewsewnewz?*
Do you have any plans ___ for today/this afternoon/tonight?	**Bugün/bugün öğleden sonra/bu akşam için planlarınız var mı?** *boogewn/boogewn ur:leden sonRa/boo aksham ichin planlaRuhnuhz vaR muh?*
Would you like to go_____ out with me?	**Benimle çıkmak ister misiniz?** *benimleh chuhkmak isteR misiniz?*
Would you like to go_____ dancing with me?	**Benimle dansa gelmek ister misiniz?** *benimleh dansa gelmek isteR misiniz?*
Would you like to have___ lunch/dinner with me?	**Benimle öğle yemeğe/akşam yemeğe çıkmak ister misiniz?** *benimleh ur:leh yeme:eh/aksham yeme:eh chuhkmak isteR misiniz?*
Would you like to come __ to the beach with me?	**Benimle plaja gelmek ister misiniz?** *benimleh plazha gelmek isteR misiniz?*
Would you like to come __ into town with us?	**Bizimle şehire inmek ister misiniz?** *bizimleh sheh-hireh inmek isteR misiniz?*
Would you like to come __ and see some friends with us?	**Bizimle arkadaşlara gelmek ister misiniz?** *bizimleh aRkadashlaRa gelmek isteR misiniz?*
Shall we dance? _____	**Dans edelim mi?** *dans edelim mi?*
– sit at the bar? _____	**Bara geliyor musun?** *baRa geliyoR moosoon?*

– get something to drink?	**Bir şeyler içmeye gidelim mi?**
	biR sheyleR ichmeyeh gidelim mi?
– go for a walk/drive? ____	**Biraz yürüyelim mi/arabayla gezelim mi?**
	biRaz yewRewyelim mi/aRabíla gezelim mi?
Yes, all right _____	**Tamam, olur**
	tamam, olooR
Good idea_____	**İyi fikir**
	iyi fikiR
No (thank you) _____	**Hayır (teşekkür ederim)**
	ha-yuhR teshek-kewR edeRim
Maybe later _____	**Belki daha sonra**
	belki da-ha sonRa
I don't feel like it _____	**Canım istemiyor**
	januhm istemiyoR
I don't have time _____	**Zamanım yok**
	zamanuhm yok
I already have a date ____	**Başka bir randevum var**
	bashka biR randevoom vaR
I'm not very good at_____ dancing/volleyball/ swimming	**Ben dansta/voleybolda/yüzmede pek iyi değilim**
	dansta/voleybolda/yewzmedeh pek iyi de:ilim

3.9 Paying a compliment

You look wonderful! _____	**Sizi çok iyi gördüm!**
	sizi chok iyi gurRdewm!
I like your car! _____	**Ne güzel araba!**
	neh gewzel aRaba!
I like your ski outfit! ____	**Ne güzel kayak kıyafeti!**
	neh gewzel ka-yak kuh-yafeti!
You're a nice boy/girl ____	**Çok iyi bir çocuksun/kızsın**
	chok iyi biR chojooksoon/kuhzsuhn
What a sweet child! _____	**Ne şirin çocuk!**
	neh shiRin chojook!

You're a wonderful _____ dancer! — **Çok güzel dans ediyorsunuz!**
chok gewzel dans ediyoRsoonooz!

You're a wonderful _____ cook! — **Çok güzel yemek pişiriyorsunuz!**
chok gewzel yemek pishiRiyoRsoonooz!

You're a terrific soccer ___ player! — **Çok iyi futbol oynuyorsunuz!**
chok iyi footbol oynooyoRsoonooz!

3.10 Chatting someone up

I like being with you _____ — **Seninle beraber olmaktan hoşlanıyorum**
seninleh beRabeR olmaktan hoshlanuhyoRoom

I've missed you so much_ — **Seni öyle özledim ki**
seni uhyleh urzledim ki

I dreamt about you _____ — **Rüyamda seni gördüm**
rew-amda seni gurRdewm

I think about you all day _ — **Bütün gün seni düşünüyorum**
bewtewn gewn seni dewshewnew-yoRoom

You have such a sweet ___ smile — **Çok tatlı gülüyorsun**
chok tatluh gewlew-yoRsoon

You have such beautiful___ eyes — **O kadar güzel gözlerin var ki**
o kadaR gewzel gurzleRin vaR ki

I'm in love with you_____ — **Sana aşığım**
sana ashuh:uhm

I'm in love with you too __ — **Ben de sana**
ben deh sana

I love you _____ — **Seni seviyorum**
seni seviyoRoom

I love you too_____ — **Ben de seni**
ben deh seni

I don't feel as strongly ___ about you — **Bu duyguları sana karşı duymuyorum**
boo dooygoolaRuh sana kaRshuh dooymoo-yoroom

I already have a _____ boyfriend/girlfriend	**Benim erkek arkadaşım/kız arkadaşım var** *benim eRkek aRkadashuhm/kuhz aRkadashum vaR*
I'm not ready for that ____	**Henüz o noktaya gelmedim** *henewz o nokta-ya gelmedim*
This is going too fast ____ for me	**Her şey çok çabuk oluyor** *heR shey chok chabook olooyoR*
Take your hands off me __	**Benden uzak dur** *benden oozak door*
Okay, no problem _____	**Tamam, sorun değil** *tamam soRoon de:il*
Will you stay with me ____ tonight?	**Bu gece bende kalır mısın?** *bu gejeh bendeh kaluhR muhsuhn?*
I'd like to go to bed ____ with you	**Seninle sevişmek istiyorum** *seninleh sevishmek istiyoRoom*
Only if we use a condom_	**Sadece prezervatif ile** *sadejeh pReseRvatif ileh*
We have to be careful ____ about AIDS	**Aids hastalığı yüzünden dikkatli olmamız gerekiyor** *ehds hastaluh:uh yewzewnden dik-katluh olmamuhz geRekiyoR*
That's what they all say __	**Herkes aynı şeyi söylüyor** *heRkes ínuh shey surlew-yor*
We shouldn't take any ____ risks	**İşi şansa bırakmayalım** *ishi shansa buhRakma-yaluhm*
Do you have a condom? _	**Prezervatifin var mı?** *pReseRvatifin vaR muh?*
No? In that case we _____ won't do it	**Yok mu? O halde sevişemeyiz** *yok moo? o haldeh sevishemeyiz*

3.11 Arrangements

When will I see _____ you again?	**Sizi tekrar ne zaman göreceğim?** *sizi tekRaR neh zaman gurReje:im?*
Are you free over the ____ weekend?	**Bu hafta sonu zamanınız var mı?** *boo hafta sonoo zamanuhnuhz vaR muh?*
What shall we arrange? __	**Nasıl yapalım?** *nasuhl yapaluhm?*
Where shall we meet? ___	**Nerede buluşalım?** *neRedeh boolooshaluhm?*
Will you pick me/us up? _	**Beni/bizi alacak mısınız?** *beni/bizi alajak muhsuhnuhz?*
Shall I pick you up? _____	**Sizi alayım mı?** *sizi ala-yuhm muh?*
I have to be home by... __	**Saat....evde olmam gerekiyor** *saht....evdeh olmam geRekiyoR*
I don't want to see _____ you anymore	**Sizi bir daha görmek istemiyorum** *sizi biR da-ha gurRmek istemiyoRoom*

3.12 Saying goodbye

Can I take you home? ___	**Sizi evinize götürebilir miyim?** *sizi evinizeh gurtewRebiliR miyim?*
Can I write/call you?_____	**Size mektup yazabilir miyim/telefon açabilir miyim?** *sizeh mektoop yazabiliR miyim/telefon achabiliR miyim?*
Will you write/call me? ___	**Bana mektup yazar mısınız/telefon açar mısınız?** *bana mektoop yazaR muhsuhnuhz/telefon achaR muhsuhnuhz?*

Can I have your _____ address/phone number?	**Adresinizi/telefon numaranızı alabilir miyim?** *adResinizi/telefon noomaRasuhnuhzuh alabiliR miyim?*
Thanks for everything ____	**Her şey için çok teşekkür ederim** *heR shey ichin chok teshek-kewR edeRim*
It was very nice _____	**Her şey çok güzeldi** *heR shey chok gewzeldi*
Say hello to... _____	**...selamlarımı söyle** *...selamlaRuhmuh suhyleh*
All the best _____	**Size her şeyin en iyisini dilerim** *sizeh heR sheyin en iyisini dileRim*
Good luck _____	**İyi şanslar** *iyi shanslaR*
When will you be back? _	**Tekrar ne zaman geleceksiniz?** *tekRaR neh zaman gelejeksiniz?*
I'll be waiting for you ____	**Sizi bekleyeceğim** *sizi bekleyeje:im*
I'd like to see you again__	**Sizi tekrar görmeyi çok isterim** *sizi tekRaR gurRmeyi chok isteRim*
I hope we meet _____ again soon	**Umarım en kısa zamanda tekrar görüşürüz** *oomaRuhm en kuhsa zamanda tekRaR gurRewshewRewz*
This is our address. _____ If you're ever in the UK...	**Bu bizim adresimiz. İngiltere'ye uğrarsanız...** *boo bizim adResimiz. ingilteRe'yeh oo:RaRsanuhz...*
...You'd be more than ___ welcome	**Her zaman bekleriz** *heR zaman bekleRiz*

4 Eating out

● **Mealtimes in Turkey** are as follows:

1. *Kahvaltı* (breakfast) – any time between 7.30 and 10am. Typically there will be bowls of olives (*zeytin*) and pieces of cheese (*beyaz peynir*) for you to nibble. There will be bread (*ekmek*) with two or three types of jam (*reçel*) or honey (*bal*). There may be spreading yoghurt (*süzme yoğurt*) – use it instead of butter, and combine it with jam. Turkish tea (*çay*) is served black, but you can ask for it to be strong (*demli*) or weak (*açık*). If you prefer, it can be drunk with lemon (*limon*) on request.

2. *Öğle yemeği* (lunch) – between 12.30 and 2.30 – often a hot meal, but lighter than supper. It is often followed by Turkish coffee, which is very strong. This can be without sugar (*şekersiz or sade*), very sweet (*şekerli*) or medium (*orta*). If you prefer just a little sugar, ask for *az şekerli*.

3. *Akşam yemeği* is the main meal of the day and it can be as early as 7pm or as late as 10pm. It usually includes a very sweet pudding (*tatlı*) but if you prefer, there is often fruit (*meyva*). Try the melon – it can be delicious. To keep you going between lunch and supper, at around 5pm you may be served a cup of tea and a pastry (*börek*).

4.1 On arrival

I'd like to book a table ___ for seven o'clock, please	**Saat yedi için bir masa ayırtabilir miyim?** *saht yedi ichin biR masa í-uhRtabiliR miyim?*
I'd like a table for two, ___ please	**İki kişilik bir masa lütfen** *iki kishilik biR masa lewtfen*
We've/we haven't booked	**Yer ayırtmıştık (ayırtmamıştık)** *yeR í-uhRtmuhshtuhk (í-uhRtmamuhshtuhk)*
Is the restaurant open ___ yet?	**Restoran açık mı?** *restoRan achuhk muh?*
What time does the ___ restaurant open/close?	**Restoran saat kaçta açılıyor/kapanıyor?** *restoRan saht kachta achuhluhyoR/kapanuhyoR?*

Yer ayırtmış mıydınız?	Do you have a reservation?
Adınız lütfen?	What name, please?
Bu taraftan lütfen	This way, please
Bu masa reserve edildi	This table is reserved
On beş dakika sonra bir masa boşalacak	We'll have a table free in fifteen minutes.
Masa boşalana kadar barda beklemek ister miydiniz?	Would you like to wait (at the bar)?

Can we wait for a table? _ **Boş bir masa için bekleyebilir miyiz?**
bosh biR masa ichin bekleyebiliR miyiz?

Do we have to wait long? **Çok beklememiz gerekiyor mu?**
chok beklememiz geRekiyoR moo?

Is this seat taken?_____ **Burası boş mu?**
booRasuh bosh moo?

Could we sit here/there? _ **Buraya/oraya oturabilir miyiz?**
booRa-ya/oRa-ya otooRabiliR miyiz?

Can we sit by the _____ **Cam kenarına oturabilir miyiz?**
window? *jam kenahRuhna otooRabiliR miyiz?*

Can we eat outside? ____ **Dışarıda da yiyebilir miyiz?**
duhshaRuhda da yiyebiliR miyiz?

Do you have another ____ **Bir sandalyeniz daha var mı?**
chair for us? *biR sandal-yeniz da-ha vaR muh?*

Do you have a highchair? **Çocuk için bir sandalyeniz var mı?**
chojook ichin biR sandal-yeniz vaR muh?

Is there a socket for ____ **Bu biberon ısıtıcısı için bir priziniz var mı?**
this bottle-warmer? *boo bibeRon uhsuhtuhjuhsuh ichin biR pRiziniz vaR muh?*

Could you warm up ____ **Bu biberonu/kavanozu ısıtabilir misiniz?**
this bottle/jar for me? *boo bibeRonoo/kavanozoo uhsuhtabiliR misiniz?*

Not too hot, please_____ **Çok sıcak olmasın lütfen**
chok suhjak olmasuhn lewtfen

Is there somewhere I ____ can change the baby's nappy?	**Bebeğin altını değiştirebileceğim bir yer var mı?**
	bebe:in altuhnuh de:ishtiRebileje:im biR yeR vaR muh?
Where are the toilets? ___	**Tuvalet ne tarafta?**
	too:alet neh taRafta?

4.2 Ordering

Waiter! _____	**Garson!**
	gaRson!
Madam! _____	**Hanımefendi!**
	hanuhmefendi!
Sir! _____	**Beyefendi!**
	beyefendi!
We'd like something to __ eat/a drink	**Bir şeyler yemek/içmek istiyoruz**
	biR sheyleR yemek/ichmek istiyoRooz
Could I have a quick ____ meal?	**Çabucak bir şeyler yiyebilir miyim?**
	chaboojak biR sheyleR yiyebiliR miyim?
We don't have much ____ time	**Fazla zamanımız yok**
	fazla zamanuhmuhz yok
We'd like to have a _____ drink first	**Önce bir şeyler içmek istiyoruz**
	uhnje biR sheyleR ichmek istiyoRooz
Could we see the _____ menu/wine list, please?	**Yemek listesini/şarap listesini rica edebilir miyim?**
	yemek listesini/shaRap listesini rija edebiliR miyim?
Do you have a menu ____ in English?	**İngilizce yemek listeniz var mı?**
	ingilizje yemek listeniz vaR muh?
Do you have a dish_____ of the day?	**Günlük menünüz/turistik menünüz var mı?**
	gewnlewk menewnewz/tooRistik menewnewz vaR muh?
We haven't made a_____ choice yet	**Henüz seçimimizi yapmadık**
	henewz sechimimizi yapmaduhk

What do you _____ recommend?	**Ne tavsiye edersiniz?**
	neh tavsiyeh edeRsiniz?
What are the specialities _ of the region/the house?	**Bu yörenin/restoranın spesyalitesi nedir?**
	boo yuhRenin/restoRanuhn spesyalitesi nediR?
I like strawberries/olives _	**Çileği/zeytini severim**
	chile:i/zeytini seveRim
I don't like meat/fish... ___	**Balığı/eti/...sevmem**
	baluh:uh/eti/...sevmem
What's this? _____	**Bu ne?**
	boo neh?
Does it have...in it? _____	**İçinde...var mı?**
	ichindeh...vaR muh?
What does it taste like? __	**Tadı neye benziyor?**
	taduh neyeh benziyoR?
Is this a hot or a _____ cold dish?	**Bu yemek sıcak mı yoksa soğuk mu?**
	boo yemek suhjak muh yoksa so:ook moo?
Is this sweet?_____	**Bu yemek tatlı mı?**
	boo yemek tatluh muh?
Is this spicy? _____	**Bu yemek acı/baharatlı mı?**
	boo yemek ajuh/bahaRatluh muh?
Do you have anything ___ else, please?	**Başka bir yemeğiniz var mı?**
	bashka biR yeme:iniz vaR muh?
I'm on a salt-free diet____	**Tuzsuz yemek perhizindeyim**
	toozsooz yemek peRhizindeyim

Aperatif alır mıydınız?	Would you like a drink first?
Seçiminizi yaptınız mı?	Have you decided?
Ne içersiniz?	What would you like to eat?
Afiyet olsun	Enjoy your meal.
Bifteğiniz nasıl olsun?	Would you like your steak rare, medium or well done?
Tatlı/kahve alır mıydınız?	Would you like a dessert/coffee?

I can't eat pork _____	**Domuz eti yemem yasak** *domooz eti yemem yasak*
– sugar _____	**Şeker kullanmam yasak** *shekeR kul-lanmam yasak*
– fatty foods _____	**Yağlı yemek yemem yasak** *ya:luh yemek yemem yasak*
– (hot) spices _____	**Baharatlı yemek yemem yasak** *bahaRatluh yemek yemem yasak*
I'll/we'll have what those people are having	**Onlarınkinin aynısını istiyorum** *onlaRuhnkinin ínuhsuhnuh istiyoRoom*
I'd like... _____	**...istiyorum** *...istiyoRoom*
We're not having a _____ starter	**Meze istemiyoruz** *mezeh istemiyoRooz*
The child will share what _ we're having	**Çocuk bizim yemeğimizden yiyecek** *chojook bizim yeme:imizden yiyejek*
Could I have some _____ more bread, please?	**Biraz daha ekmek getirir misiniz lütfen?** *biRaz da-ha ekmek getiRiR misiniz lewtfen?*
– a bottle of water/wine _	**Bir şişe su/şarap getirir misiniz lütfen?** *biR shisheh su/shaRap getiRiR misiniz lewtfen?*
– another helping of... _	**Bir porsiyon...getirir misiniz lütfen?** *biR poRsiyon...getiRiR misiniz lewtfen?*
– some salt and pepper_	**Tuz ve karabiber getirir misiniz lütfen?** *tooz ve kaRabibeR getiRiR misiniz lewtfen?*
– a napkin _____	**Bir peçete getirir misiniz lütfen?** *biR pecheteh getiRiR misiniz lewtfen?*
– a spoon _____	**Bir kaşık getirir misiniz lütfen?** *biR kashuhk getiRiR misiniz lewtfen?*
– an ashtray _____	**Bir kül tablası getirir misiniz lütfen?** *biR kewl tablasuh getiRiR misiniz lewtfen?*
– some matches _____	**Bir kutu kibrit getirir misiniz lütfen?** *biR kootoo kibrit getiRiR misiniz lewtfen?*
– some toothpicks _____	**Birkaç tane kürdan getirir misiniz lütfen?** *biRkach taneh kewRdan getiRiR misiniz lewtfen?*

– a glass of water _____	**Bir bardak su getirir misiniz lütfen?**
	biR baRdak soo getiRiR misiniz lewtfen?
– a straw (for the child) __	**(Çocuk için) bir kamış getirir misiniz lütfen?**
	(chojook ichin) biR kamuhsh getiRiR misiniz lewtfen?
Enjoy your meal! _____	**Afiyet olsun!**
	afiyet olsoon!
You too!_____	**Size de!**
	sizeh deh!
Cheers! _____	**Şerefe!**
	sheRefeh!
The next round's on me__	**Bir dahaki sefer sıra bende**
	biR da-haki sefeR suhRa bendeh
Could we have a doggy__ bag, please?	**Kalanları paket yapar mısınız?**
	kalanlaRuh paket yapaR muhsuhnuhz?

4.3 The bill

See also 8.2 Settling the bill

How much is this dish? __	**Bu yemeğin fiyatı ne kadar?**
	boo yeme:in fiyatuh neh kadaR?
Could I have the bill, ____ please?	**Hesap lütfen**
	hesap lewtfen
All together_____	**Hepsi bir arada**
	hepsi biR aRada
Everyone pays separately	**Herkes kendi hesabını ödeyecek**
	heRkes kendi hesabuhnuh urdeyejek
Could we have the menu again, please?	**Yemek listesine bir göz atabilir miyiz?**
	yemek listesine biR gurz atabiliR miyiz?
The...is not on the bill____	**...hesapta yok**
	...hesapta yok

4.4 Complaints

It's taking a very long time	**Çok uzun sürüyor**	
	chok oozoon sewRew-yor	
We've been here an hour already	**Bir saatten beri buradayız**	
	biR saht-ten beRi booRada-yuhz	
This must be a mistake __	**Bir yanlışlık olmalı**	
	bir yanluhshluhk olmaluh	
This is not what I ordered	**Ben bunu ısmarlamamıştım**	
	ben boonoo uhsmaRlamamuhshtuhm	
I ordered... _____	**...istemiştim**	
	...istemishtim	
There's a dish missing __	**Yemeklerden biri eksik**	
	yemekleRden biRi eksik	
This is broken/not clean _	**Bu kırık/kirli**	
	boo kuhRuhk/kiRli	
The food's cold _____	**Yemek soğuk**	
	yemek so:ook	
– not fresh _____	**Yemek taze değil**	
	yemek tazeh de:il	
– too salty/sweet/spicy _	**Yemek çok tuzlu/tatlı/baharatlı**	
	yemek chok toozloo/tatluh/bahaRatluh	
The meat's not done ____	**Et iyi pişmemiş**	
	et iyi pishmemish	
– overdone _____	**Et çok haşlanmış**	
	et chok hashlanmuhsh	
– tough _____	**Et çok sert**	
	et chok seRt	
– off _____	**Et bozuk**	
	et bozook	
Could I have something else instead of this?	**Bunun yerine bana başka bir şey verebilir misiniz?**	
	boonoon yeRineh bana bashka biR shey veRebiliR misiniz?	

The bill/this amount is ___ not right	**Hesapta bir yanlışlık var**
	hesapta bir yanluhshluhk vaR
We didn't have this_____	**Biz bunu yemedik**
	biz boonoo yemedik
There's no paper in the __ toilet	**Tuvalette tuvalet kağıdı kalmamış**
	too-alet-te too-alet ka:uhduh kalmamuhsh
Do you have a _____ complaints book?	**Şikayet defteriniz var mı?**
	shika-yet defteRiniz vaR muh?
Will you call the_____ manager, please?	**Şefinizi çağırır mısınız lütfen?**
	shefinizi cha:uhRuhR muhsuhnuhz lewtfen?

4.5 Paying a compliment

That was a wonderful____ meal	**Yemeklerinizi çok beğendik**
	yemekleRinizi chok be:endik
The food was excellent __	**Yemekleriniz çok lezizdi**
	yemekleRiniz chok lezizdi
The...in particular was ___ delicious	**Özellikle...çok lezzetliydi**
	urzel-likleh...chok lez-zetliydi

4.6 The menu

alkollü içkiler
alcoholic drinks

alkolsüz içkiler
non-alcoholic drinks

aperatif aperitif

balık çeşitleri
choice of fish dishes

çorba çeşitleri
choice of soups

etli yemekler
meat dishes

etsiz yemekler
vegetarian dishes

ızgara grills

kahvaltı breakfast

KDV dahil
including VAT

kokteyller cocktails

menü menu

meyva fruit

mezeler starters

pasta çeşitleri
choice of cakes

salatalar salads

şarap listesi
wine list

sebze yemekleri
vegetable dishes

servis dahil
service included

servis hariç
service not included

sıcak yemekler
hot dishes

soğuk yemekler
cold dishes

tatlılar
sweets (puddings)

4.7 Alphabetical list of drinks and dishes

alabalık
trout

armut pear

aşure
sweet dish made from
fruit and many kinds
of nut

ayran
yoghurt drink

ayşe kadın fasulyesi
green beans

ayva
quince

badem ezmesi
ground almonds

bakla
broad beans

baklava
sticky pastry

balık fish

beyaz peynir
white cheese (like feta)

beyaz şarap
white wine

bezelye
peas

biber
peppers

biber dolması
stuffed peppers

biftek
steak

bira
beer

bisküvi
biscuits

böbrek kidneys

bonfile
best cut (beef)

börek	**dil**	**etli bezelye**
pastry	tongue	peas cooked with
brüksel lahanası	**dil balığı**	meat
Brussels sprouts	sole	**fasulye**
bulgur	**domates**	beans
bulgar wheat	tomatoes	**fındık**
but	**domates çorbası**	hazelnuts
leg (of meat)	tomato soup	**fırında**
buz	**domates dolması**	oven-roast
ice	stuffed tomatoes	**gazoz**
cacık	**domates salatası**	fizzy lemonade
cucumber and yoghurt	tomato salad	**güveç**
çay	**domates salçası**	meat and vegetable
tea	sauce made from	casserole
çerkez tavuğu	tomatoes	**hamsi**
chicken with walnuts	**domuz eti**	anchovy
ceviz	pork	**hardal**
walnut	**dondurma**	mustard
ciğer	ice cream	**havuç**
liver	**döner**	carrot
çikolata	spit-roast	**helva**
chocolate	**düğün çorbası**	halva
çikolatalı dondurma	meat and yoghurt	**hindi**
chocolate ice cream	soup	turkey
çilek	**ekmek** bread	**hurma**
strawberries	**elma**	dates
cızbız köfte	apple	**iç pilav**
grilled meatballs	**enginar**	rice stuffing
çoban salatası	globe artichoke	**imam bayıldı**
cucumber, tomato and	**erik**	stuffed aubergine
onion salad	plum	**incir** fig
çorba	**et**	**irmik helvası**
soup	meat	semolina helva
dana eti	**et suyu**	**işkembe çorbası**
veal	meat stock	tripe soup

ıspanak
spinach

ıstakoz
lobster

istiridye oysters

ızgara
grill/grilled

izmir köftesi
meatballs in tomato
  sauce

jöle
jelly

kabak
courgettes/marrow

kabak dolması
stuffed courgettes

kadınbudu köfte
meat and rice rissoles

kahve
coffee

kalkan balığı
turbot

karabiber
black pepper

karides
shrimps

karışık
mixed

karnabahar
cauliflower

karnıyarık
aubergine stuffed with
  minced meat

karpuz
water melon

kaşar peyniri
cheese (cheddar-
  type, sometimes
  dry, usually
  mature)

kavun
melon

kayısı
apricot

kebap
kebab

keçi
goat

kekik
thyme

keklik
partridge

kereviz
celery

kestane
chestnut

ketçap
ketchup

kiraz
cherry

kırlangıç
swallow (bird)

kırmızı biber
red pepper

kırmızı lahana
red cabbage

kırmızı şarap
red wine

kırmızı turp
radishes

kıyma
mince

kızartılmış ekmek
toast

köfte
meat-balls

kokoreç
sheep's chitterlings
  cooked on a spit

komposto
stewed fruit

koyun eti
mutton

kuru fasulye
dried beans

kuşkonmaz
asparagus

kuzu budu
leg of lamb

kuzu eti
lamb

lahana
cabbage

lahana dolması
stuffed cabbage

lahmacun
Turkish pizza made
  with minced meat,
  spices and onions

levrek
bass

limon
lemon

limonata
lemonade

lokum
Turkish delight
maden sodası
soda water
maden suyu
mineral water
makarna
macaroni
mandalina
tangerine, mandarin
mantar
mushroom
maydanoz
parsley
mayonez
mayonnaise
menemen
omlette with tomatoes,
 onion and paprika
mercimek çorbası
lentil soup
meyva suyu
fruit juice
mezgit
whiting
midye
mussels
midye dolması
stuffed mussels
midye pilakisi
mussel stew (cold)
midye tava
fried mussels
mısır
sweetcorn

mücver
courgette croquettes
mürekkep balığı
squid
muz
banana
nar
pomegranate
omlet
omlette
ördek
duck
pancar
beetroot
pastırma
pressed (spiced)
 meat
patates
potatoes
patates kızartması
chips
patates püresi
mashed potatoes
patates salatası
potato salad
patlıcan
aubergine
patlıcan kızartması
fried aubergine
patlıcan musakkası
moussaka
patlıcan salatası
aubergine salad
peynir
cheese

pide
(flat) bread
pilav
rice
piliç
small chicken
pırasa
leek
pirzola
cutlet
portakal
orange
portakal suyu
orange juice
rafadan yumurta
lightly-
 boiled egg
rakı
aniseed spirit served
 mixed with a little
 water
ringa balığı
herring
roka
rocket (salad
 vegetable)
salata salad
salatalık
cucumber
salmon
salmon
şam fıstığı
pistachio
şarap
wine

sardalya
sardines
sarımsak
garlic
sazan carp
sebze
vegetable
sebze çorbası
vegetable soup
şeftali
peach
şeker sugar
şekerpare
small cakes cooked in
  sweet syrup
sığır eti
beef
sirke
vinegar
şiş kebap
sish kebab
sivri biber
long green pepper
siyah zeytin
black olives
sos sauce
su water
süt
milk
tarçın
cinnamon
tarhana çorbası
soup made from grain,
  yoghurt and
  tomatoes

tas kebabı
braised lamb
tavada fried
tavşan rabbit
tavuk chicken
tavuk çorbası
chicken soup
tavuk göğsü
milk pudding
  cooked with
  chicken breast
taze
fresh
terbiyeli
with a sauce
tereyağı
butter
tereyağlı
made with butter
turna balığı
pike
turp
radishes
turşu
pickled
tuz salt
tuzlu
with added salt, salty
tuzsuz
without salt
un
flour
un kurabiyesi
cake made with
  almond and nuts

uskumru
mackerel
üzüm
grapes
vanilya
vanilla
vanilyalı dondurma
vanilla ice-cream
vermut
vemouth
viski
whisky
vişne
morello cherries
yağlı et
meat (not lean)
yağsız et
lean meat
yaprak dolması
stuffed vine leaves
yayla çorbası
parsley and yoghurt
  soup
yengeç
crab
yeşil zeytin
green olives
yoğurt yoghurt
yoğurt çorbası
yoghurt soup
yumurta eggs
zeytin olives
zeytin yağı olive oil
zeytin yağlı
made with olive oil

5.1 Asking for directions

Excuse me, could I ask you something?	**Özür dilerim, size bir şey sorabilir miyim?** *urzewR dileRim, sizeh biR shey soRabiliR miyim?*
I've lost my way	**Yolumu kaybettim** *yoloomoo kíbet-tim*
Is there a(n)... around here?	**Bu civarda bir...var mı?** *boo jivaRda biR...vaR muh?*
Is this the way to...?	**...giden yol bu mu?** *...giden yol boo moo?*
Could you tell me how to get to the... (name of place) by car/on foot?	**Bana...arabayla/yaya nasıl gidebileceğimi söyleyebilir misiniz?** *bana...aRabíla/ya-ya nasuhl gidebileje:imi suhyleyebiliR misiniz?*
What's the quickest way to...?	**...en çabuk nasıl gidebilirim?** *...en chabook nasuhl gidebiliRim?*
How many kilometres is it to...?	**...kaç kilometre kaldı?** *...kach kilometReh kalduh?*
Could you point it out on the map?	**Haritada gösterebilir misiniz?** *haRitada gursteRebiliR misiniz?*

Bilmiyorum, buralı değilim	I don't know, I don't know my way around here
Yanlış yoldasınız	You're going the wrong way
... geri dönmelisiniz	You have to go back to...
Oradan levhaları takip ediniz	From there on just follow the signs
Oraya varınca tekrar sorun	When you get there, ask again

doğru	kavşak	ırmak/nehir
straight ahead	the intersection	the river
sola	**sokak**	**bağlantı yolu**
left	the street	the flyover
sağa	**trafik ışıkları**	**köprü**
right	the traffic lights	the bridge
dönmek	**tünel** the tunnel	**hemzemin geçit**
turn	**'yol ver' işareti**	the level crossing/the
takip etmek	the `give way' sign	boom gates
follow	**bina** the building	... **giden yolu**
karşıya geçmek	**köşede**	**gösteren levha**
cross	at the corner	the sign pointing to...

5.2 Customs

● **Before you set out**, you will need a valid passport. On arrival, you will have to acquire a visa, which is normally issued automatically. Queue for the visa before passport control. Drivers need an international driving licence, green card, UK plates, insurance which is valid in Turkey and also their car registration documents. You may take 5 litres of spirits into the country, and up to 200 cigarettes.

My children are entered ___ **Çocuklar pasaportuma kayıtlı**
on this passport *chojooklaR pasapoRtooma kayuhtluh*

I'm travelling through ____ **Ülkenizden geçiyordum**
ewlkenizden gechiyoRdoom

I'm going on holiday to...___ **...tatile gidiyorum**
...tatileh gidiyoRoom

I'm on a business trip____ **İş seyahatindeyim**
ish sey-ahatindeyim

I don't know how long ___ **Ne kadar kalacağımı daha bilmiyorum**
I'll be staying yet *neh kadaR kalaja:uhmuh da-ha*
 bilmiyoRoom

Pasaportunuz lütfen	Your passport, please
Yeşil kartınız lütfen	Your green card, please
Araba ruhsatınız lütfen	Your vehicle documents, please
Vizeniz lütfen	Your visa, please
Nereye gidiyorsunuz?	Where are you heading?
Ne kadar kalmayı düşünüyorsunuz?	How long are you planning to stay?
Beyan edecek bir şeyiniz var mı?	Do you have anything to declare?
Bunu açar mısınız?	Open this, please

I'll be staying here for____ **Bir hafta sonu kalacağım**
a weekend *biR hafta sonoo kalaja:uhm*

– for a few days_____ **Birkaç gün kalacağım**
 biRkach gewn kalaja:uhm

– for a week _____ **Bir hafta kalacağım**
 biR hafta kalaja:uhm

– for two weeks_____ **İki hafta kalacağım**
 iki hafta kalaja:uhm

I've got nothing to_____ **Beyan edecek bir şeyim yok**
declare *bey**ahn** edejek biR sheyim yok*

I've got...with me _____ **Yanımda...var**
 yanuhmda...vaR

– ...cartons of cigarettes _ **Yanımda bir karton sigara var**
 yanuhmda biR kaRton sigaRa vaR

– ...bottles of..._____ **Yanımda bir şişe...var**
 yanuhmda biR shisheh...vaR

– some souvenirs _____ **Yanımda birkaç hediyelik eşya var**
 yanuhmda biRkach hediyelik eshya vaR

These are personal _____ **Bunlar benim şahsi eşyalarım**
effects *boonlaR benim shasi eshyalaRuhm*

These are not new _____ **Bu eşyalar yeni değil**
 boo eshyalaR yeni de:il

Here's the receipt _____ **Makbuzu burada**
 makboozoo booRada

This is for private use ____	**Bu kişisel kullanım için**
	boo kishisel kool-lanuhm ichin
How much import duty __ do I have to pay?	**Ne kadar gümrük vergisi ödemem gerek?**
	neh kadaR gewmRewk veRgisi urdemem geRek?
Can I go now? _____	**Gidebilir miyim?** _gidebiliR miyim?_

5.3 Luggage

Porter! _____	**Hamal!**
	hamal!
Could you take this_____ luggage to...?	**Bu bagajı...götürür müsünüz lütfen?**
	boo bagazhuh...gurtewRewR mewsewnewz lewtfen?
How much do I _____ owe you?	**Borcum ne kadar?**
	boRjoom neh kadaR?
Where can I find a_____ luggage trolley?	**Nerede bir bagaj vagonu bulabilirim?**
	neRedeh biR bagazh vagonoo boolabiliRim?
Could you store this _____ luggage for me?	**Bu bagajı emanete verebilir miyim?**
	boo bagazhuh em**ahneteh** veRebiliR miyim?
Where are the luggage___ lockers?	**Bagaj saklama dolapları nerede?**
	bagazh saklama dolaplaRuh neRedeh?
I can't get the locker ____ open	**Bagaj saklama dolabını açamıyorum**
	bagazh saklama dolabuhnuh achamuhyoRoom
How much is it per item _ per day?	**Parça başına günlüğü ne kadar?**
	paRcha bashuhna gewnlew:ew neh kadaR?
This is not my bag/_____ suitcase	**Bu benim çantam/bavulum değil**
	boo benim chantam/bavooloom de:il
There's one item/bag/ ___ suitcase missing still	**Bir parça/çanta/bavul eksik**
	biR paRcha/chanta/bavool eksik
My suitcase is damaged _	**Bavulum hasara uğramış**
	bavooloom hasaRa oo:Ramuhsh

5.4 Traffic signs

Beklemek yasaktır	**H (hastane)**	**Tamirat**
no waiting	H (hospital)	roadworks
Bozuk yol	**Havaalanı**	**Tek yön**
poor road surface	airport	one way
D (durak)	**Jandarma**	**Tünel**
D (bus stop)	gendarmarie	tunnel
Dikkat	**Park etmek yasaktır**	**Viraj**
caution	no parking	bend
Dur	**Polis**	**Yangın tehlikesi**
stop	police	danger of fire
Gümrük	**Şehir merkezi**	**Yavaş**
customs	city centre	slow

5.5 The car

● **Speed limits** are 50km/h in built-up areas and 90km/h on the open road (for cars with trailers, limits are 40 and 70 respectively).
All accidents must be reported to the police whether or not personal injury occurs. In the event of an accident, you may find the other driver has *tek taraflı* insurance which covers only his or her own claims, or *çift taraflı* which should cover yours, too.
In country areas, Turkish drivers are always on the look-out for the occasional unexpected obstruction on the road (farm machinery or herds of animals) and in the towns, when the traffic lights show green, they may well prudently check that no car is about to cross their path against the red. Turkish driving standards are often high, but always be ready for exceptions.
On open roads, *take particular care on bends, as adverse cambers are not unknown.*

The parts of a car

battery	**akümülatör**	*akewmewlaturR*
rear light	**arka lamba**	*aRka lamba*
rear-view mirror	**ayna**	*ína*
reversing light	**geri vites lambası**	*geRi vites lambasuh*
aerial	**anten**	*anten*
car radio	**radyo**	*radyo*
petrol tank	**yakıt deposu**	*yakuht deposoo*
inside mirror	**iç ayna**	*ich ína*
sparking plugs	**buji**	*boozhi*
fuel filter/pump	**yakıt filtresi/pompası**	*yakuht filtResi/pompasuh*
wing mirror	**dış ayna**	*duhsh ína*
bumper	**tampon**	*tampon*
carburettor	**karbüratör**	*kaRbewRaturR*
crankcase	**karter**	*kaRteR*
cylinder	**silindir**	*silindiR*
ignition	**kontak**	*kontac*
warning light	**kontrol lambası**	*kontRol lambasuh*
dynamo	**dinamo**	*dinamo*
accelerator	**gaz pedalı**	*gaz pedaluh*
handbrake	**el freni**	*el fReni*
valve	**subap**	*soobap*
silencer	**ses kesici**	*ses kesiji*
boot	**bagaj**	*bagazh*
headlight	**far**	*faR*
crank shaft	**krank**	*kRank*
air filter	**hava filtresi**	*hava filtResi*
fog lamp	**sis lambası**	*sis lambasuh*
engine block	**motorblok**	*motoRblok*
camshaft	**kamlı mil**	*kamluh mil*
oil filter/pump	**yağ filtresi/pompası**	*ya: filtResi/pompasuh*
dipstick	**yağ seviye kontrol** **çubuğu**	*ya: seviyeh kontRol* *chooboo:oo*

pedal	pedal	*pedal*
door	kapı	*kapuh*
radiator	radyatör	*rad-yaturR*
brake disc	fren diski	*fRen diski*
spare wheel	yedek tekerlek	*yedek tekeRlek*
indicator	yön gösterici	*yurn gursteRiji*
windscreen wiper	cam sileceği	*jam sileje:i*
shock absorbers	amortisör	*amoRtisurR*
sunroof	tente	*tenteh*
spoiler	arka kapak	*aRka kapak*
starter motor	marş motoru	*maRsh motoRoo*
steering column	direksiyon kutusu	*diReksiyon kootoosoo*
exhaust pipe	egzoz borusu	*egzoz boRoosoo*
seat belt	emniyet kemeri	*emniyet kemeRi*
fan	vantilatör	*vantilaturR*
distributor cables	distribütör kablosu	*distRibewturR kablosoo*
gear lever	vites kolu	*vites koloo*
windscreen	ön cam	*urn jam*
water pump	su pompası	*soo pompasuh*
wheel	tekerlek	*tekeRlek*
hubcap	tekerlek poyrası	*tekeRlek poyRasuh*
piston	piston	*piston*

5.6 The petrol station

● **Petrol is not particularly expensive** in Turkey, and out-of town filling stations often have excellent facilities for refreshment. Attendant service is normal.

How many kilometres to _ the next petrol station, please?	**Bir sonraki benzin istasyonuna kaç kilometre var?** *biR sonRaki benzin istas-yonoona kach kilometReh vaR?*
I would like...litres of..., _ please	**...litre...istiyorum** *...litReh...istiyoRoom*
– super _____	**...litre kurşunlu benzin istiyorum** *...litReh kooRshoonloo benzin istiyoRoom*
– leaded _____	**...litre kurşunsuz benzin istiyorum** *...litReh kooRshoonsooz benzin istiyoRoom*
– unleaded _____	**...litre süper benzin istiyorum** *...litReh sewpeR benzin istiyoRoom*
– diesel _____	**...litre dizel istiyorum** *...litReh dizel istiyoRoom*
I would like...liras' _____ worth of petrol, please	**...liralık benzin istiyorum** *...liRaluhk benzin istiyoRoom*
Fill her up, please _____	**Doldurun lütfen** *doldooRoon lewtfen*
Could you check...? _____	**...kontrol eder misiniz?** *...kontRol edeR misiniz?*
– the oil level _____	**Yağ seviyesini kontrol eder misiniz?** *ya: seviyesini kontRol edeR misiniz?*
– the tyre pressure _____	**Lastiklerdeki hava basıncını kontrol eder misiniz?** *lastikleRdeki hava basuhnjuhnuh kontRol edeR misiniz?*
Could you change the ___ oil, please?	**Yağı değiştirebilir misiniz?** *ya:uh de:ishtiRebiliR misiniz?*

| Could you clean the _____ windows/the windscreen, please? | **Camları/ön camı silebilir misiniz?** *jamlaRuh/on camuh silebiliR misiniz?* |
| Could you give the car____ a wash, please? | **Arabamı yıkayabilir misiniz?** *aRabamuh yuhka-yabiliR misiniz?* |

5.7 Breakdown and repairs

I'm having car trouble. ___ Could you give me a hand?	**Arabam arızalandı. Yardım edebilir misiniz?** *aRabam aRuhzalanduh. yaRduhm edebiliR misiniz?*
I've run out of petrol_____	**Benzinim bitti** *benzinim bit-ti*
I've locked the keys _____ in the car	**Anahtarları arabanın içinde unuttum** *anaHtaRlaRuh aRabanuhn ichindeh oonoot-toom*
The car/motorbike/_____ moped won't start	**Arabam/motosikletim/mopetim çalışmıyor** *aRabam/motosikletim/mopetim chalushmuhyoR*
Could you contact the ___ recovery service for me, please?	**Benim için Türkiye Turing ve Otomobil Kurumunu arayabilir misiniz?** *benim ichin tewRkiyeh tooRing ve otomobil kooRoomoonu ara-yabiliR misiniz?*
Could you call a garage___ for me, please?	**Bir araba tamircisini arayabilir misiniz?** *biR aRaba **tah**miRcisini aRa-yabiliR misiniz?*
Could you give me _____ a lift to...?	**Sizinle...kadar gelebilir miyim?** *sizinleh...kadaR gelebiliR miyim?*
– a garage/into town? ___	**Sizinle bir araba tamircisine/şehire kadar gelebilir miyim?** *sizinleh biR aRaba **tah**miRjisineh/she-hiReh kadaR gelebiliR miyim?*

– a phone booth? _____	**Sizinle bir telefon kulübesine kadar gelebilir miyim?** *sizinleh biR telefon koolewbesineh kadaR gelebiliR miyim?*
– an emergency phone? _	**Sizinle en yakın telefona kadar gelebilir miyim?** *sizinleh en yakuhn telefona kadaR gelebiliR miyim?*
Can we take my _____ bicycle/moped?	**Bisikletimi/mobiletimi de alabilir miyiz?** *bisikletimi/mobiletimi deh alabiliR miyiz?*
Could you tow me to ____ a garage?	**Arabamı bir araba tamircisine kadar çekebilir misiniz?** *aRabamuh biR aRaba tahmiRjisineh kadaR chekebiliR misiniz?*
There's probably _____ something wrong with...(See 68–69)	**Büyük bir olasılıkla...arızalı** *bewyewk biR olasuhluhkla...aRuhzaluh*
Can you fix it? _____	**Tamir edebilir misiniz?** *tahmiR edebiliR misiniz?*
Could you fix my tyre? ___	**Lastiğimi tamir edebilir misiniz?** *lasti:imi tahmiR edebiliR misiniz?*
Could you change this ___ wheel?	**Bu tekerleği değiştirebilir misiniz?** *boo tekeRle:i de:ishtiRebiliR misiniz?*
Can you fix it so it'll _____ get me to...?	**...varana kadar idare edecek bir şekilde tamir edebilir misiniz?** *...vaRana kadaR idaReh edejek biR shekildeh tahmiR edebiliR misiniz?*
Which garage can_____ help me?	**Bana hangi tamircide yardımcı olabilirler?** *bana hangi tahmiRjideh yaRduhmjuh olabiliRleR?*
When will my car/bicycle_ be ready?	**Arabam/bisikletim ne zaman hazır olur?** *aRabam/bisikletim neh zaman hazuhR olooR?*
Can I wait for it here?____	**Burada bekleyebilir miyim?** *booRada bekleyebiliR miyim?*
How much will it cost? __	**`Ne kadar tutacak?** *neh kadaR tootajak?*

Could you itemise_____ the bill?	**Hesabı makbuza ayrıntılı olarak geçirebilir misiniz?**
	hesabuh makbooza íRuhntuhluh olaRak gechiRebiliR misiniz?
Can I have a receipt for __ the insurance?	**Sigorta için bir makbuz verir misiniz?**
	sigoRta ichin biR makbooz veRiR misiniz?

5.8 The bicycle/moped

● **Turks use bicycles** only for short-distance journeys, and cycling by tourists is only gradually becoming more common.
Motorcycles are subject to the same speed limits as cars with trailers (40km/h in town and 70 on the open road).

5.9 Renting a vehicle

I'd like to rent a... _____	**...kiralamak istiyorum**
	...kiRalamak istiyoRoom
Do I need a (special)_____ licence for that?	**Onun için (özel) bir ehliyetim olması gerekiyor mu?**
	onoon ichin (urzel) biR eHliyetim olmasuh geRekiyoR moo?
I'd like to rent the...for...__	**... ...kiralamak istiyorum**
	... ...kiRalamak istiyoRoom
– one day _____	**...bir günlüğüne kiralamak istiyorum**
	...biR gewnlew:ewneh kiRalamak istiyoRoom
– two days _____	**...iki günlüğüne kiralamak istiyorum**
	...iki gewnlew:ewneh kiRalamak istiyoRoom
How much is that per____ day/week?	**Günlüğü/haftalığı ne kadar?**
	gewnlew:ew/haftaluh:uh neh kadaR?
How much is the_____ deposit?	**Ne kadar kaparo ödemem gerek?**
	neh kadaR kapaRo urdemem geRek?

Could I have a receipt ___ for the deposit?

Sizden kaparoyu ödediğime dair bir makbuz alabilir miyim?

sizden kapaRoyu urdedi:ime díR biR makbooz alabiliR miyim?

How much is the _____ surcharge per kilometre?

Kilometre başına ek olarak ne kadar ödemem gerek?

kilometReh bashuhnuh ek olaRak neh kadaR urdemem geRek?

Does that include petrol?

Benzin dahil mi?

benzin da-hil mi?

Does that include _____ insurance?

Sigorta dahil mi?

sigoRta da-hil mi?

What time can I pick ____ the...up tomorrow?

...yarın saat kaçta gelip alabilirim?

...yaRuhn saht kachta gelip alabiliRim?

When does the...have ____ to be back?

...ne zaman geri getirmem gerek?

...neh zaman geRi getiRmem geRek?

Where's the petrol tank? _

Yakıt deposu nerede?

yakuht deposoo neRedeh?

Arabanız/bisikletiniz için gerekli yedek parçalar elimde yok	I don't have parts for your car/bicycle
Yedek parçaları başka bir yerden almam gerek	I have to get the parts from somewhere else
Yedek parçaları ısmarlamam gerek	I have to order the parts
Yarım gün sürer	That'll take half a day
Bir gün sürer	That'll take a day
Birkaç gün sürer	That'll take a few days
Bir hafta sürer	That'll take a week
Arabanız hurda olmuş	Your car is a write-off
Yapılacak hiç bir şey yok	It can't be repaired
Arabanız/motosikletiniz/mobiletiniz/bisikletiniz saat...hazır olur	The car/motor bike/moped/bicycle will be ready at...o'clock

What sort of fuel does it take?	**Depoyu hangi tür yakıt ile doldurmam gerek?**
	depoyoo hangi tewR yakuht ileh doldooRmam geRek?

5.10 Hitchhiking

● **Short-distance hitch-hiking** is very common in Turkey, but you will be expected to offer to pay the driver (*Borcum ne kadar?*). As a visitor, your offer will almost certainly be declined, but it is rude not to make the gesture.

For long distances, check out the bus prices. They can be surprisingly inexpensive, just as much a social opener, and much more dependable than hitching.

Where are you heading?	**Nereye gidiyorsunuz?**
	neReyeh gidiyoRsoonooz?
Can I come along?	**Sizinle gelebilir miyim?**
	sizinleh gelebiliR miyim?
Can my boyfriend/ girlfriend come too?	**Erkek/kız arkadaşım da gelebilir mi?**
	eRkek/kuhz aRkadashuhm da gelebiliR mi?
I'm trying to get to...	**...gitmem gerek**
	...gitmem geRek
Is that on the way to...?	**...yolu üzerinde mi?**
	...yoloo ewzeRindeh mi?
Could you drop me off...?	**Beni...indirebilir misiniz?**
	beni...indiRebiliR misiniz?
– here?	**Beni burada indirebilir misiniz?**
	beni booRada indiRebiliR misiniz?
– at the...exit?	**Beni...giden yolda indirebilir misiniz?**
	beni...giden yolda indiRebiliR misiniz?
– in the centre?	**Beni şehir merkezinde indirebilir misiniz?**
	beni she-hiR meRkezindeh indiRebiliR misiniz?

The parts of a bicycle

rear lamp	**arka lamba**	*aRka lamba*
rear wheel	**arka tekerlek**	*aRka tekeRlek*
(luggage) carrier	**port bagaj**	*poRt bagazh*
fork crown	**direksiyon mili**	*diReksiyon mili*
bell	**zil**	*zil*
inner tube	**iç lastik**	*ich lastik*
tyre	**dış lastik**	*duhsh lastik*
crank	**pedal kolu**	*pedal koloo*
gear change	**zincir dişlisi**	*zinjiR dishlisi*
wire	**kablo**	*kablo*
dynamo	**dinamo**	*dinamo*
bicycle trailer	**iki tekerlek yük arabası**	*iki tekeRlek yewk aRabasuh*
frame	**karkas**	*kaRkas*
dress guard	**çamurluk**	*chamooRlook*
	(bayan elbisesi için)	*(ba-yan elbisesi ichin)*
chain	**zincir**	*zinjiR*
chain guard	**zincir muhafazası**	*zinjiR moohafazasuh*
lock and chain	**zincir kiliti**	*zinjiR kiliti*
milometer	**kilometre sayacı**	*kilometReh sa-yajuh*
child's seat	**çocuk oturacağı**	*hojook otooRaja:uh*
headlamp	**far**	*faR*
bulb	**ampul**	*ampool*
pedal	**pedal**	*pedal*
pump	**bisiklet pompası**	*bisiklet pompasuh*
reflector	**reflektör**	*reflekturR*

– at the next roundabout?	**Beni bir sonraki dönel kavşakta indirebilir misiniz?**
	beni biR sonRaki durnel kavshakta indiRebiliR misiniz?
Could you stop here, ___ please?	**Burada durur musunuz lütfen?**
	booRada dooRooR moosoonooz lewtfen?

break pad	fren kampanası	*fRen kampanasuh*
brake cable	fren teli	*fRen teli*
ring lock	dairesel kilit	*díResel kilit*
carrier straps	bagaj lastiği	*bagazh lastik*
speedometer	hız göstergesi	*huhz gursteRgesi*
spoke	jant teli	*zhant teli*
mudguard	çamurluk	*chamooRlook*
handlebar	direksiyon	*diReksiyon*
chain wheel	çark	*chaRk*
toe clip	tutma aleti	*tootma aleti*
crank axle	pedal kolu mili	*pedal koloo mili*
drum brake	makaralı fren	*makaRaluh fRen*
rim	jant	*zhant*
valve	subap	*subap*
valve sleeve	subap hortumu	*subap hoRtoomoo*
gear cable	vites teli	*vites teli*
front fork	ön tekerlek çatalı	*urn tekeRlek chataluh*
front wheel	ön tekerlek	*urn tekeRlek*
seat	sele	*seleh*

I'd like to get out here ___	**Burada inmek istiyorum**
	booRada inmek istiyoRoom
How much do I owe you?	**Borcum ne kadar?**
	borjoom neh kadaR?
Thanks for the lift _____	**Otostop için teşekkür ederim**
	otostop ichin teshek-kewR edeRim

6.1 In general

● **Train travel** is not the automatic option for long-distance travel. The rail network is relatively restricted, and journey times can be very long. Bus travel, on the other hand, is surprisingly cheap and very efficient, so ask first about bus timetables and fares, and check out competing companies. The bus-station (*otogar*) may be on the edge of town, but a minibus service often provides a city-centre link. Seats are numbered, and bookable in advance; you would do well to avoid the sunny side of the bus.

Your fellow-passengers will be friendly, and ensure that you get off at the stop you want. Each bus has an attendant (*yardımcı*) and the upmarket companies provide a hostess (*hostes*). The *yardımcı* or *hostes* will provide cologne for passengers to splash on their hands and hair, and, when asked, will give anyone water to drink. Refreshment breaks come every hour and a half.

Announcements

...giden (10:40) treninin...5 dakika rötarı var	The [10:40] train to...has been delayed by 15 minutes
...giden/...gelen (10:40) tren 5. perona girmek üzeredir	The train now arriving at platform 5 is the [10:40] train to.../from...
...giden (10:40) tren 5. peronda hala bekliyor	The [10:40] train to...is about to leave from platform 5
...giden tren...perondan hareket etmektedir	The train to...will leave from platform...
...istasyonuna girmek üzereyiz	We're now approaching...

Where does this train ____ go to?	**Bu tren nereye gidiyor?**
	boo tRen neReyeh gidiyoR?
Does this boat go to...? ____	**Bu vapur...gidiyor mu?**
	boo vapooR...gidiyoR moo?
Can I take this bus to...? ____	**...gitmek için bu otobüse mi binmem gerekiyor?**
	...gitmek ichin boo otobewseh mi binmem geRekiyoR?
Does this train stop at...?	**Bu tren...duruyor mu?**
	boo tRen...dooRooyoR moo?
Is this seat taken/free/ ____ reserved?	**Burası dolu mu/boş mu/ayırtılmış mı?**
	booRasuh doloo moo/bosh moo/a-yuhRtuhlmuhsh muh?
I've booked... _____	**Ben...yer ayırtmıştım**
	ben...yeR a-yuhRtmuhshtuhm
Could you tell me _____ where I have to get off for... ?	**Nerede inmem gerektiğini söyler misiniz?**
	neRedeh inmem geRekti:ini suhyleR misiniz?
Could you let me_____ know when we get to...?	**...geldiğimizde beni uyarır mısınız?**
	...geldi:imizdeh beni ooy-aRuhR muhsuhnuhz?
Could you stop at the ____ next stop, please?	**Bir sonraki durakta durur musunuz lütfen?**
	biR sonRaki dooRakta dooRooR moosoonooz lewtfen?
Where are we now? _____	**Neredeyiz?**
	neRedeyiz?
Do I have to get off here?	**Burada mı inmem gerekiyor?**
	booRada muh inmem geRekiyoR?
Have we already _____ passed...?	**...geçtik mi?**
	...gechtik mi?
How long have I been ____ asleep?	**Ne kadar uyumuşum?**
	neh kadaR ooy-oomooshoom?
How long does... _____ stop here?	**...burada ne kadar kalacak?**
	...booRada neh kadaR kalajak?

Can I come back on the __ same ticket?	**Bu bilet dönüşte de geçerli mi?**
	boo bilet durnewshteh deh gecheRli mi?
Can I change on this ____ ticket?	**Bu biletle aktarma yapabilir miyim?**
	boo biletleh aktaRma yapabiliR miyim?
How long is this ticket __ valid for?	**Bu bilet ne zamana kadar geçerli?**
	boo bilet neh zamana kadaR gecheRli?

6.2 Questions to passengers

Ticket types

Birinci sınıf mı yoksa ikinci sınıf mı?	First or second class?
Tek gidiş mi yoksa gidiş dönüş mü?	Single or return?
Sigara içilir mi içilmez mi?	Smoking or non-smoking?
Cam kenarına mı koridor tarafına mı?	Window or aisle?
Ön tarafa mı yoksa arka tarafa mı?	Front or back?
Koltuk mu kuşet mi?	Seat or couchette?
Üstte mi, ortada mı yoksa altta mı?	Top, middle or bottom?
Turistik sınıf mı yoksa birinci sınıf mı?	Tourist class or business class?
Kamara mı yoksa koltuk mu?	Cabin or seat?
Tek kişilik mi yoksa iki kişilik mi?	Single or double?
Kaç kişisiniz?	How many are travelling?

6.3 Tickets

Destination

Nereye gidiyorsunuz?	Where are you travelling?
Ne zaman yola çıkacaksınız?	When are you leaving?
...saat...kalkıyor	Your...leaves at...
Aktarma yapmanız gerek	You have to change trains
...inmeniz gerek	You have to get off at...
...yoluyla seyahat etmeniz gerek	You have to travel via...
Gidiş...	The outward journey is on...
Dönüş...	The return journey is on...
En geç...binmiş olamanız gerekiyor	You have to be on board by...

Inside the vehicle

Biletiniz lütfen	Your ticket, please
Yer ayırdığınızı gösteren belge lütfen	Your reservation, please
Pasaportunuz lütfen	Your passport, please
Yanlış yere oturmuşsunuz	You're in the wrong seat
Yanlış ... binmişsiniz	You're on/in the wrong...
Bu yer ayırtılmıştır	This seat is reserved
Bir miktar ek olarak ödemeniz gerekiyor	You'll have to pay a supplement
... ...dakika rötarlı	The...has been delayed by...minutes

Where can I ...?	Nerede...?
	neRedeh...?
– buy a ticket?	**Nerede bir bilet satın alabilirim?**
	neRedeh biR bilet satuhn alabiliRim?
– make a reservation?	**Nerede bir yer ayırtabilirim?**
	neRedeh biR yeR a-yuhRtabiliRim?
– book a flight?	**Nerede bir uçak bileti ayırtabilirim?**
	neRedeh biR oochak bileti a-yuhRtabiliRim?
Could I have a...to...., please?	... ...istiyorum
	... ...istiyoRoom
– a single	...tek gidiş istiyorum
	...tek gidish istiyoRoom
– a return	...gidiş dönüş istiyorum
	...gidish durnewsh istiyoRoom
first class	**birinci sınıf**
	biRinji suhnuhf
second class	**ikinci sınıf**
	ikinji suhnuhf
tourist class	**turistik sınıf**
	tooRistik suhnuhf
business class	**Birinci sınıf**
	biRinji suhnuhf
I'd like to book a seat/couchette/cabin	**Bir koltuk/kuşet/kamara ayırtmak istiyorum**
	biR koltook/kooshet/kamaRa a-yuhRtmak istiyoRoom
I'd like to book a berth in the sleeping car	**Kuşetli bir yer ayırtmak istiyorum**
	kooshetli biR yeR a-yuhRtmak istiyoRoom
top/middle/bottom	**üst/orta/alt**
	ewst/oRta/alt
smoking/no smoking	**sigara içilir/içilmez**
	sigaRa ichiliR/ichilmez
by the window	**cam kenarına**
	jam kenaRuhna

single/double _____	**tek kişilik/iki kişilik**
	tek kishilik/iki kishilik
at the front/back _____	**ön tarafta/arka tarafta**
	urn taRafta/aRka taRafta
There are...of us _____	**... kişiyiz**
	... kishiyiz
a car _____	**Bir araba ileyiz**
	biR aRaba ileyiz
a caravan _____	**Bir karavan ileyiz**
	biR kaRavan ileyiz
...bicycles _____	**...bisiklet ileyiz**
	...bisiklet ileyiz
Do you also have...? _____	**...var mı?**
	...vaR muh?
– season tickets? _____	**Abone biletiniz de var mı?**
	aboneh biletiniz deh vaR muh?
– weekly tickets? _____	**Haftalık abone biletiniz de var mı?**
	haftaluhk aboneh biletiniz deh vaR muh?
– monthly season	**Aylık abone biletiniz de var mı?**
tickets?	*íluhk aboneh biletiniz deh vaR muh?*

6.4 Information

Where's? _____	**...nerede?**
	...neRedeh?
Where's the information _____	**Danışma bürosu nerede?**
desk?	*danuhshma bewRosoo neRedeh?*
Where can I find a _____	**Tren/otobüs tarifesi nerede?**
timetable?	*tRen/otobews taRifesi neRedeh?*
Where's the...desk? _____	**...gişesi nerede?**
	...gishesi neRedeh
Do you have a city map _____	**şehrin otobüs/metro ağını gösteren bir**
with the bus/the	**haritanız var mı?**
underground routes on	*sheHRin otobews/metRo a:uhnuh*
it?	*gursteRen biR haRitanuhz vaR muh?*

Do you have a _____ train/bus timetable?	**Tren/otobüs tarifeniz var mı?** *tRen/otobews taRifeniz vaR muh?*
I'd like to confirm/_____ cancel/change my booking for/trip to...	**...olan rezervasyonumu/yolculuğumu konfirme etmek/iptal etmek/değiştirmek istiyorum** *...olan rezeRvasyonoomoo/ yoljooloo:oomoo konfriRmeh etmek/iptahl etmek/de:ishtiRmek istiyoRoom*
Will I get my money _____ back?	**Paramı geri alabilir miyim?** *paRamuh geRi alabiliR miyim?*
I want to go to... _____ How do I get there? (What's the quickest way there?)	**...gitmek istiyorum. (En çabuk) nasıl gidebilirim?** *...gitmek istiyoRoom. (en chabook) nasuhl gidebiliRim?*
How much is a _____ single/return to...?	**...tek gidiş/gidiş dönüş ne kadar?** *...tek gidish/gidish durnewsh neh kadaR?*
Do I have to pay a _____ supplement?	**Ek olarak bir şey ödemem gerekiyor mu?** *ek olaRak biR shey urdemem geRekiyoR moo?*
Can I interrupt my _____ journey with this ticket?	**Bu biletle yolculuğuma ara verebilir miyim?** *boo biletleh yoljooloo:ooma aRa veRebiliR miyim?*
How much luggage _____ am I allowed?	**Yanıma ne kadar bagaj alabilirim?** *yanuhma neh kadaR bagazh alabiliRim?*
Can I send my luggage _____ in advance?	**Bagajlarımı önceden gönderebilir miyim?** *bagazhlaRuhmuh urnjeden gurndeRebiliR miyim?*
Does this...travel direct? _____	**Bu...dosdoğru mu gidiyor?** *boo...dosdo:Roo moo gidiyoR?*
Do I have to change? _____ Where?	**Aktarma yapmam gerekiyor mu? Nerede?** *aktaRma yapmam geRekiyoR moo? neRedeh?*
Will there be any _____ stopovers?	**Uçak aktarmalı uçuş mu yapıyor?** *oochak aktaRmaluh oochoosh moo yapuhyoR?*

Does the boat call in at any ports on the way?	**Bu vapur yolculuk sırasında başka limanlara da uğruyor mu?**
	boo vapooR yoljoolook suhRasuhnda bashka limanlaRa da oo:RooyoR moo?
Does the train/bus stop at...?	**Bu tren/otobüs...duruyor mu?**
	boo tRen/otobews...dooRooyoR moo?
Where should I get off?	**Nerede inmem gerekiyor?**
	neRedeh inmem geRekiyoR?
Is there a connection to...?	**...giden araca hemen aktarma yapmam mümkün mü?**
	...giden aRaja hemen aktaRma yapmam mewmkewn mew?
How long do I have to wait?	**Ne kadar beklemem gerekiyor?**
	neh kadaR beklemem geRekiyoR?
When does...leave?	**...ne zaman kalkıyor?**
	...neh zaman kalkuhyoR?
What time does the first/next/last...leave?	**İlk/bir sonraki/en son...saat kaçta kalkıyor?**
	ilk/biR sonRaki/en son...saht kachta kalkuhyoR?
How long does...take?	**Yolculuk kaç saat sürüyor?**
	yoljoolook kach saht sewRew-yoR?
What time does...arrive in...?	**...saat kaçta...varıyor?**
	...saht kachta...vaRuh-yoR?
Where does the...to...leave from?	**...giden...nereden kalkıyor?**
	...giden...neReden kalkuh-yoR?
Is this...to...?	**...giden...bu mu?**
	...giden...boo muh?

6.5 Aeroplanes

● **At arrival at a Turkish airport** (*havaalanı*), you will find the
following signs:

geliş arrivals	**iç hatlar**	**dış hatlar**
gidiş	domestic flights	international
departures		

6.6 Trains

● **If you prefer** train to bus, be sure to choose the express trains
(*mavi tren, ekspres, or mototren*). Avoid the 'passenger' (*yolcu*) or mail
(*posta*) trains, as these can be astonishingly slow.
When reading timetables, remember that the station name, not the
city name, will generally be used. If in doubt, ask.

6.7 Taxis

● **The regular taxis** are not the only option. Ask about the *dolmuş*
service. These follow a pre-set route, but can be flagged down (or
will allow you to get off) at any point on the way. They are either
minibuses or big old cars, and have a distinctive yellow stripe.
If you do take a regular taxi, just be sure the driver starts his meter as
you get in. If he forgets, remind him ('*Taksimetreyi açar mısınız*'). It may
save a lot of argument later. The Turks themselves do not normally
expect to tip taxi drivers, and you are quite within your rights to
refuse. However, since foreign travellers do so often offer tips, you
could volunteer one if you wished. Don't feel coerced, though.

boş	**dolu**	**taksi durağı**
for hire	booked	taxi rank

Taxi! _____	**Taksi!**
	taksi!
Could you get me a taxi, _ please?	**Benim için bir taksi çağırabilir misiniz?**
	benim ichin biR taksi cha:uhRabiliR misiniz?
Where can I find a taxi ___ around here?	**Bu civarda nerede bir taksi bulabilirim?**
	boo jivaRda neRedeh biR taksi boolabiliRim?
Could you take me to..., _ please?	**Beni...götürün lütfen**
	beni...gurtewRewn lewtfen
– this address _____	**Beni bu adrese götürün lütfen**
	beni boo adReseh gurtewRewn lewtfen
– the...hotel _____	**Beni...oteline götürün lütfen**
	beni...otelineh gurtewRewn lewtfen
– the town/city centre ___	**Beni şehir merkezine götürün lütfen**
	beni shehiR meRkezineh gurtewRewn lewtfen
– the station _____	**Beni istasyona götürün lütfen**
	beni istas-yona gurtewRewn lewtfen
– the airport _____	**Beni havaalanına götürün lütfen**
	beni hava-alanuhna gurtewRewn lewtfen
How much is the_____ trip to...?	**...gitmek ne kadar tutar?**
	...gitmek neh kadaR tootaR?
How far is it to...? _____	**...kaç kilometre?**
	...kach kilometReh?
Could you turn on the ___ meter, please?	**Taksimetreyi açar mısınız lütfen?**
	taksimetReyi achaR muhsuhnuhz lewtfen?
I'm in a hurry _____	**Acelem var**
	ajelem vaR
Could you speed up/ ____ slow down a little?	**Daha hızlı/yavaş gidebilir misiniz?**
	da-ha huhzluh/yavash gidebiliR misiniz?
Could you take a_____ different route?	**Başka bir yoldan gidebilir misiniz?**
	bashka biR yoldan gidebiliR misiniz?
I'd like to get out here, ___ please.	**Beni burada indirin, lütfen**
	beni booRada indiRin lewtfen

You have to go...here ____	**Buradan...gidin/dönün**
	booRadan...gidin/durnewn
You have to go straight __ on here	**Buradan doğru gidin**
	booRadan do:Roo gidin
You have to turn left ____ here	**Buradan sola dönün**
	booRadan sola durnewn
You have to turn right____ here.	**Buradan sağa dönün**
	booRadan sa:a durnewn
This is it _____	**Burası**
	booRasuh
Could you wait a minute _ for me, please?	**Bir saniye bekler misiniz?**
	*biR **sah**niyeh bekleR misiniz?*

7 Overnight accomodation

7.1 General

● **There is a five star rating system** for hotels, with luxury hotels
exactly the same as in any other country. Two or three star hotels can
provide all the facilities expected by most European travellers, and
offer a more than adequate standard of comfort.
Prices can be very reasonable indeed.
If you have enough money to spare, ask for information about hotels
in former Ottoman mansions. They can be outstanding for their
exotic atmosphere, and can be a memorable part of your stay. By
Turkish standards they are not cheap, however. For those who need
to be careful with money, a bed-and-breakfast *pansiyon* will offer a
perfectly adequate place to stay. Even cheaper (but not very
attractive) accommodation can be found in a hostel (*yurt*) or student
hostel (*öğrenci yurdu*).
There are also camp-sites (with varying facilities) but mostly these are
located in the major tourist areas.

Ne kadar kalacaksınız?	How long will you be staying?
Bu formu doldurur musunuz lütfen?	Fill in this form, please
Pasaportunuzu görebilir miyim?	Could I see your passport?
Kaparo ödemeniz gerek	I'll need a deposit
Peşin olarak ödemeniz gerek	You'll have to pay in advance

My name's...I've made __ a reservation over the phone/by mail	**Adım...(telefonla/yazılı olarak) yer ayırtmıştım** *aduhm...(telefonla/yazuhluh olaRak) yeR a- yuhRtmuhshtuhm*
How much is it per _____ night/week/ month?	**Bir geceliği/haftalığı/aylığı ne kadar?** *biR gejeli:i/haftaluh:uh/iluh:uh neh kadaR?*

We'll be staying at _____ least...nights/weeks	**En az...gece/hafta kalacağız** *en az...gejeh/hafta kalaja:uhz*
We don't know yet _____	**Tam olarak bilmiyoruz** *tam olaRak bilmiyoRooz*
Do you allow pets _____ (cats/dogs)?	**Ev hayvanlarını (kedi/köpek) kabul ediyor musunuz?** *ev hívanlaRuhnuh (kedi/kurpek) kabool ediyoR moosoonooz?*
What time does the _____ gate/door open/close?	**Demir parmaklık/kapı saat kaçta açılıyor/kapanıyor?** *demiR paRmakluhk/kapuh saht kachta achuhluhyoR/kapanuhyoR?*
Could you get me _____ a taxi, please?	**Benim için bir taksi çağırır mısınız?** *benim ichin biR taksi cha:uhRuhR muhsuhnuhz?*
Is there any mail _____ for me?	**Bana posta var mı?** *bana posta vaR muh?*

7.2 Camping

Where's the manager? _____	**Yönetici nerede?** *yurnetiji neRedeh?*
Are we allowed to _____ camp here?	**Burada kamp kurabilir miyiz?** *booRada kamp kooRabiliR miyiz?*
There are...of us and _____ ...tents	**...kişi ve...çadırlayız** *...kishi veh...chaduhRla-yuhz*
Can we pick our _____ own pitch?	**Çadır kurabileceğimiz yeri kendimiz seçebilir miyiz?** *chaduhR kooRabileje:imiz yeRi kendimiz sechebiliR miyiz?*
Do you have a quiet _____ spot for us?	**Bizim için sakin bir yeriniz var mı?** *bizim ichin **sak**in biR yeRiniz vaR muh?*
Do you have any other _____ pitches available?	**Başka boş yeriniz yok mu?** *bashka bosh yeRiniz vaR muh?*

Yerinizi kendiniz seçebilirsiniz	You can pick your own site
Yeriniz gösterilecek	You'll be allocated a site
Yer numaranız bu	This is your site number
Bunu arabanıza yapıştırır mısınız?	Stick this on your car, please
Lütfen, bu kartı kaybetmeyiniz	Please don't lose this card

It's too windy/sunny/ ____ shady here.	**Burası çok rüzgarlı/güneşli/gölgeli** *booRasuh chok rewzgaRluh/gewneshli/gurlgeli*
It's too crowded here ____	**Burası çok kalabalık** *booRasuh chok kalabaluhk*
The ground's too____ hard/uneven	**Yer çok sert/pürüzlü** *yeR chok seRt/pewRewzlew*
Do you have a level ____ spot for the camper/caravan/folding caravan?	**Minibüs/karavan/açılır kapanır karavan için düz bir yeriniz var mı?** *minibews/kaRavan/achuhluhR kapanuhR kaRavan ichin dewz biR yeRiniz vaR muh?*
Could we have adjoining ____ pitches?	**Yan yana iki yer alabilir miyiz?** *yan yana iki yeR alabiliR miyiz?*
Can we park the car____ next to the tent?	**Arabayı çadırın yanına park edebilir miyiz?** *aRaba-yuh chaduhRuhn yanuhna paRk edebiliR miyiz?*
How much is it per ____ person/tent/caravan/ car?	**Kişi/çadır/karavan/araba başına ne kadar tutar?** *kishi/chaduhR/kaRavan/aRaba bashuhnuh neh kadaR tootaR?*
Are there any cabins for ____ hire?	**Kiralık kulübeniz var mı?** *kiRaluhk koolewbeniz vaR muh?*

Camping equipment

luggage space	bagaj yeri	*bagazh yeRi*
can opener	konserve açacağı	*konseRveh achaja:uh*
butane gas bottle	tüp gaz	*tewp gaz*
pannier	bisiklet çantası	*bisiklet chantasuh*
gas cooker	tüp ocağı	*tewp oja:uh*
groundsheet	zemin örtüsü	*zemin urRtewsew*
mallet	çekiç	*chekich*
hammock	hamak	*hamak*
jerry can	bidon	*bidon*
campfire	kamp ateşi	*kamp ateshi*
folding chair	portatif sandalye	*poRtatif sandalyeh*
insulated picnic box	termos kutusu	*teRmos kootoosoo*
ice pack	paket buz	*paket booz*
compass	pusula	*poosoola*
(incandescent) gas mantle	_ lamba gömleği	*lamba gurmle:i*
corkscrew	tirbuşon	*tiRbooshon*
airbed	şişirme yatak	*shishiRmeh yatak*
airbed plug	şişirme yatak hava tıpası	*shishiRmeh yatak hava tuhpasuh*
pump	pompa	*pompa*
awning	güneşlik	*gewneshlik*
karimat	döşek	*durshek*
pan	tencere	*tenjeReh*
pan handle	kap kacak tutacağı	*kap kajak tootaja:uh*
primus stove	parafin ocağı	*parafin oja:uh*
zip	fermuar	*feRmoo-aR*
backpack	sırt çantası	*suhRt chantasuh*
guy rope	germe ipi	*geRmeh ipi*

sleeping bag	uyku tulumu	*ooykoo tooloomoo*
storm lantern	gemici feneri	*gemiji feneRi*
camp bed	portatif kamp yatağı	*poRtatif kamp yata:uh*
table	masa	*masa*
tent	çadır	*chaduhR*
tent peg	çadır kazığı	*chaduhR kazuh:uh*
tent pole	çadır direği	*chaduhR diRe:i*
vacuum flask	termos	*teRmos*
water bottle	portatif su bidonu	*poRtatif soo bidonoo*
clothes peg	mandal	*mandal*
clothes line	çamaşır ipi	*chamashuhR ipi*
windbreak	rüzgarlık	*rewzgaRluhk*
torch	el feneri	*el feneRi*
pocket knife	çakı	*chakuh*

Are there any...?	...var mı? ...vaR muh?
– hot showers?	Duşlar sıcak sulu mu? dooshlaR suhjak sooloo moo?
– washing machines?	Çamaşır makinesi var mı? chamashuhR makinesi vaR muh?
Is there a...on the site?	Bu arazide bir...var mı? boo aRahzideh biR...vaR muh?
Is there a children's play area on the site?	Bu arazide bir çocuk bahçesi var mı? boo aRahzideh biR chocook baHjesi vaR muh?
Are there covered cooking facilities on the site?	Bu arazide bir mutfak var mı? boo aRahzideh biR mootfak vaR muh?
Can I rent a safe here?	Burada bir kasa kiralayabilir miyim? booRada biR kasa kiRalayabiliR miyim?
Are we allowed to barbecue here?	Burada mangal yakabilir miyiz? booRada mangal yakabiliR miyiz?
Are there any power points?	Elektrik bağlantısı var mı? elektRik ba:lantuhsuh vaR muh?
Is there drinking water?	İçme suyu var mı? ichmeh soo-yoo vaR muh?
When's the rubbish collected?	Çöp ne zaman alınıyor? churp neh zaman aluhnuhyoR?
Do you sell gas bottles (butane gas/propane gas)?	Tüp gaz (bütan/propan) satıyor musunuz? tewp gaz (bewtan/pRopan) satuhyoR moosoonooz?

7.3 Hotel/B&B/apartment/holiday house

Do you have a _____ single/double room available?	**Tek/iki kişilik boş odanız var mı?** *tek/iki kishilik bosh odanuhz vaR muh?*
per person/per room ____	**kişi başına/oda başına** *kishi bashuhna/oda bashuhna*
Does that include _____ breakfast/lunch/dinner?	**Kahvaltı/öğle yemeği/akşam yemeği dahil mi?** *kaHvaltuh/ur:leh yeme:i/aksham yeme:i dah-hil mi?*
Could we have two_____ adjoining rooms?	**Yanyana iki odanız var mı?** *yanyana iki odanuhz vaR muh?*
with/without _____ toilet/bath/shower	**tuvaletli/tuvaletsiz/banyolu/banyosuz/ duşlu/duşsuz** *too-aletli/too-aletsiz/banyoloo/banyosooz/ dooshloo/dooshsooz*
(not) facing the street ____	**sokağa bakan (bakmayan)** *soka:a bakan (bakma-yan)*
with/without a view_____ of the sea	**deniz manzaralı/deniz manzarası olmayan** *deniz manzaRaluh/deniz manzaRasuh olma-yan*
Is there...in the hotel?____	**Otelde...var mı?** *oteldeh...vaR muh?*
Is there a lift in the _____ hotel?	**Otelde asansör var mı?** *oteldeh asansurR vaR muh?*

Tuvalet ve duş aynı katta/odanızda mevcut	You can find the toilet and shower on the same floor/en suite
Bu taraftan lütfen	This way, please
Odanız...katta, oda numaranız...	Your room is on the...floor, number...

Do you have room service?	**Otelde oda servisi var mı?**
	oteldeh oda seRvisi vaR muh?
Could I see the room? ___	**Odayı görebilir miyim?**
	odayuh gurRebilir miyim?
I'll take this room_____	**Bu odayı tutuyorum**
	boo odayuh tootooyoRoom
We don't like this one____	**Bunu beğenmedik**
	boonoo be:enmedik
Do you have a larger/____ less expensive room?	**Daha büyük/ucuz bir odanız var mı?**
	da-ha bew-yewk biR odanuhz vaR muh?
Could you put in a cot? __	**Odaya bir çocuk karyolası yerleştirebilir misiniz?**
	odaya biR chojook kaR-yolasuh yeRleshtiRebiliR misiniz?
What time's breakfast? __	**Kahvaltı saat kaçta?**
	kaHvaltuh saht kachta?
Where's the dining _____ room?	**Yemek salonu ne tarafta?**
	yemek salonoo neh taRafta?
Can I have breakfast ____ in my room?	**Kahvaltıyı odamda edebilir miyim?**
	kaHvaltuh odamda edebiliR miyim?
Where's the emergency __ exit/fire escape?	**Acil çıkış/yangın merdiveni ne tarafta?**
	***ah-jil** chukuhsh/yan-guhn meRdiveni neh taRafta?*
Where can I park my ____ car (safely)?	**Arabamı nereye emniyetle park edebilirim?**
	aRabamuh neReyeh emniyetleh paRk edebiliRim?
The key to room..., _____ please	**...numaralı odanın anahtarı lütfen**
	...noomaRuhluh odanuhn anaHtaRuh lewtfen
Could you put this in ____ the safe, please?	**Bunu emanete verebilir miyim?**
	*boonoo em**ahn**eteh veRebiliR miyim?*
Could you wake me _____ at...tomorrow?	**Beni yarın saat...uyandırır mısınız?**
	beni yaRuhn saht...ooy-anduhRuhR muhsuhnuhz?
Could you find a _____ babysitter for me?	**Bana bir çocuk bakıcısı bulabilir misiniz?**
	bana biR chojook bakuhjuhsuh boolabiliR misiniz?

Could I have an extra___ blanket?	Fazladan bir battaniyeniz var mı?
	fazladan biR bat-taniyeniz vaR muh?
What days do the _____ cleaners come in?	Haftanın hangi günleri temizlik yapılıyor?
	haftanuhn hangi gewnleRi temizlik yapuhluhyoR?
When are the sheets/___ towels/tea towels changed?	Çarşaflar/havlular/mutfak bezleri ne zaman değiştiriliyor?
	chaRshaflaR/havloolaR/mutfak bezleRi neh zaman de:ishtiRiliyoR?

7.4 Complaints

We can't sleep for_____ the noise	Gürültüden uyuyamıyoruz
	gewRewltewden ooy-ooy-amuhyoRooz
Could you turn the _____ radio down, please?	Radyonun sesini biraz kısar mısınız?
	radyonun sesini biRaz kuhsaR muhsuhnuhz?
We're out of toilet paper _	Tuvalet kağıdı bitmiş
	too-alet ka:uhduh bitmish
There aren't any.../there's not enough...	Hiç/yeterince...yok
	hich/yeteRinjeh...yok
The bed linen's dirty_____	Çarşaflar kirli
	chaRshaflaR kiRli
The room hasn't been ___ cleaned.	Oda temizlenmemiş
	oda temizlenmemish
The kitchen is not clean__	Mutfak temiz değil
	mootfak temiz de:il
The kitchen utensils are__ dirty	Mutfak eşyaları pis
	mootfak eshyalaRuh pis
The heater's not _____ working	Kalorifer çalışmıyor
	kaloRifeR chaluhshmuhyoR
There's no (hot) _____ water/electricity	(Sıcak) su akmıyor/elektrikler kesik
	(suhjak) soo akmuh-yoR/elektRikleR kesik
...is broken _____	...bozuk
	...bozook

Could you have that ____ seen to?	**Onu yaptırabilir misiniz?** *onoo yaptuhRabiliR misiniz?*
Could I have another ____ room/site?	**Başka bir oda/çadır için başka bir yer istiyorum** *bashka biR oda/chaduhR ichin bashka biR yeR istiyoRoom*
The bed creaks terribly __	**Yatak çok gıcırdıyor** *yatak chok guhjuhRduhyoR*
The bed sags_____	**Yatak çok çöküyor** *yatak chok churkew-yoR*
There are bugs/insects __ in our room	**Döşeğin altına koyabileceğim bir tahtanız var mı?** *Durshe:in altuhna koyabileje:im bir taHtanuhz vaR muh?*
This place is full_____ of mosquitos	**Burası sivrisinek dolu** *booRasuh sivRisinek doloo*
– cockroaches _____	**Burası hamam böceği dolu** *booRasuh hamam burje:i doloo*
– Brits _____	**Burası İngilizlerle dolu** *booRasuh ingilizleRleh doloo*

See also 8.2 Settling the bill

I'm leaving tomorrow.____ Could I settle my bill, please?	**Yarın yola çıkıyorum. Hesabı ödeyebilir miyim?** *yaRuhn yola chuhkuhyoRoom. hesabuh urdeyebiliR miyim?*
What time should we ____ vacate?	**...saat kaçta boşaltmamız gerek?** *...saht kachta boshaltmamuhz geRek?*
Could I have my deposit/ passport back, please?	**Kaparoyu/pasaportumu geri verir misiniz?** *kapaRo-yoo/pasapoRtoomoo geRi veRiR misiniz?*
We're in a terrible hurry __	**Çok acelemiz var** *chok ajelemiz vaR*
Could you forward ____ my mail to this address?	**Bana gelen mektupları bu adrese yollayabilir misiniz?** *bana gelen mektooplaRuh boo adReseh yol-la-yabiliR misiniz?*
Could we leave our____ luggage here until we leave?	**Yola çıkana kadar bavullarımızı buraya bırakabilir miyiz?** *yola chuhkana kadaR bavool-laRuhmuhzuh booRaya buhRakabiliR miyiz?*
Thanks for your _____ hospitality	**Misafirperverliğinize çok teşekkür ederim** *misahfiRpeRveRli:inizeh chok teshek-kewR edeRim*

Money matters

● **Before you travel** (or at the airport when you arrive), change just a 'survival' amount of UK currency into TL, as you will probably get a better rate at the high-street exchange offices. (These are, incidentally, quicker and have fewer formalities than banks.) You should be given a receipt. Keep all receipts carefully, as you could be asked to show them at border crossings to justify purchases made in Turkey.

Banks – if you need them – are open from 8.30 or 9 through to 12 or 12.30, then from 1.30 to 5 or 5.30. They are closed on Saturdays.

8.1 Banks

Where can I find a_____ bank/an exchange office around here?	**Bu civarda nerede bir banka/kambiyo bürosu var?** *boo jivaRda neRedeh biR banka/kambiyo bewRosoo vaR?*
Where can I cash this____ traveller's cheque/giro cheque?	**Bu seyahat/posta çekini nerede bozdurabilirim?** *boo seya-hat/posta chekini neRedeh bozdooRabiliRim?*
Can I cash this...here? ___	**Bu...burada bozdurabilir miyim?** *boo...booRada bozdooRabiliR miyim?*
Can I withdraw money____ on my credit card here?	**Burada kredi kartıyla para çekebilir miyim?** *booRada kRedi kaRtuhyla paRa chekebiliR miyim?*
What's the minimum/ _____ maximum amount?	**En az/en fazla ne kadar çekebilirim?** *en az/en fazla neh kadaR chekebiliRim?*
Can I take out less _____ than that?	**Bundan daha az para çekebilir miyim?** *boondan da-ha az paRa chekebiliR miyim?*
I've had some money____ transferred here. Has it arrived yet?	**Adıma para transfer edilmişti. Geldi mi acaba?** *aduhma paRa tRansfeR edilmishti. geldi mi ajaba?*

These are the details of __ my bank in the UK	**Bunlar benim İngiltere'deki bankamın verileri**
	boonlaR benim ingilteRedeki bankamuhn veRileRi
This is my bank/giro _____ number	**Bu benim banka hesabımın/posta çeki hesabımın numarası**
	boo benim banka hesabuhmuhn/posta cheki hesabuhmuhn noomaRasuh
I'd like to change _____ some money	**Para bozdurmak istiyorum**
	paRa bozdooRmak istiyoRoom
– pounds into... _____	**...steRlin...**
	...steRlin...
– dollars into... _____	**...dola ...**
	...dolaR...
What's the exchange ____ rate?	**Günlük döviz kuru ne kadar?**
	gewnlewk durviz kooRoo neh kadaR?
Could you give me _____ some small change with it?	**Bir kısmını bozuk para olarak verebilir misiniz?**
	biR kuhsmuhnuh bozook paRa olaRak veRebiliR misiniz?
This is not right _____	**Bir yanlışlık olmalı**
	biR yanluhshluhk olmaluh

Burayı imzalayın	Sign here, please
Bunu doldurun	Fill this out, please
Pasaportunuzu görebilir miyim?	Could I see your passport, please?
Nüfus cüzdanınızı görebilir miyim?	Could I see some identification, please?
Posta çeki kartınızı görebilir miyim?	Could I see your girobank card, please?
Banka kartınızı görebilir miyim?	Could I see your bank card, please?

8.2 Settling the bill

Could you put it on___ my bill?	**Hesabıma geçirebilir misiniz?** *hesabuhma gechiRebiliR misiniz?*
Does this amount ___ include service?	**(Bu hesaba) servis dahil mi?** *(boo hesaba) seRvis **dah**-hil mi?*
Can I pay by...? ___	**ile ödeyebilir miyim...?** *ileh urdeyebiliR miyim...?*
Can I pay by credit card?	**Kredi kartı ile ödeyebilir miyim?** *kRedi kaRtuh ileh urdeyebiliR miyim?*
Can I pay by traveller's ___ cheque?	**Seyahat çeki ile ödeyebilir miyim?** *seya-hat cheki ileh urdeyebiliR miyim?*
Can I pay with foreign ___ currency?	**Döviz ile ödeyebilir miyim?** *durviz ileh urdeyebiliR miyim?*
You've given me too___ much/you haven't given me enough change	**Paranın üstünü fazla/eksik verdiniz** *paRanuhn ewstewnew fazla/eksik veRdiniz*
Could you check this ___ again, please?	**Bunu bir daha hesaplar mısınız?** *boonoo biR da-ha hesaplaR muhsuhnuhz?*
Could I have a receipt, ___ please?	**Bana bir makbuz/fiş verebilir misiniz?** *bana biR makbooz/fish veRebiliR misiniz?*
I don't have enough ___ money on me	**Yanımda yeterince para yok** *yanuhmda yeteRinjeh paRa yok*
This is for you ___	**Buyurun, bu sizin** *booyooRoon, boo sizin*
Keep the change___	**Paranın üstü kalsın** *paRanuhn ewstew kalsuhn*

Kredi kartı/seyahat çeki/döviz kabul etmiyoruz	We don't accept credit cards/traveller's cheques/foreign currency

Post and telephone

9.1 Post

For giros, see 8 Money matters

● **Post offices** The central post offices in cities (PTTs) are open from 8am till 8pm, or even later, Monday to Saturday, and from 9 till 7 on Sundays. Smaller post offices are open for normal business hours. Postal services are comparable with those on offer throughout Europe. Delivery times are a little slower than in some countries, but are by no means the slowest in Europe.

havale	pul	telgraf
money order	stamps	telegrams
paketler		
parcels		

Where's...? _____	**...nerede?**
	...neRedeh?
Where's the post office? _	**Bu civarda nerede bir postane var?**
	boo jivaRda neRedeh biR postaneh vaR?
Where's the main post office? ___	**Merkez postane nerede?**
	meRkez postaneh neRedeh?
Where's the postbox? ___	**Bu civarda nerede bir posta kutusu var?**
	boo jivaRda neRedeh biR posta kootoosoo vaR?
Which counter should I go to...? ___	**Hangi gişede...?**
	hangi gishedeh...?
– to send a fax_____	**Hangi gişede faks çektirebilirim?**
	hangi gishedeh faks chektiRebiliRim?
– to change money_____	**Hangi gişede para bozdurabilirim?**
	hangi gishedeh paRa bozdooRabiliRim?

– to change giro cheques	**Hangi gişede posta çeki bozdurabilirim?**
	hangi gishedeh posta cheki bozdooRabiliRim?
– for a Telegraph Money _ Order?	**Hangi gişede havale çektirebilirim?**
	hangi gishedeh havaleh chektiRebiliRim?
Poste restante _____	**Postrestant**
	postRestant
Is there any mail for me. _ My name's...	**Bana posta var mı? Adım...**
	bana posta vaR muh? aduhm...

Stamps

What's the postage_____ for a...to...?	**...gidecek...için kaç liralık posta pulu yapıştırmam gerek?**
	...gidejek...ichin kach liRaluhk posta pooloo yapuhshtuhRmam geRek?
Are there enough _____ stamps on it?	**Yeterince pul yapıştırmış mıyım?**
	yeteRinjeh pool yapuhshtuhRmuhsh muhyuhm?
I'd like... ...Lira stamps___	**...liralık...tane posta pulu istiyorum**
	...liRaluhk...taneh posta pooloo istiyoRoom
I'd like to send this... ____	**Bunu...yollamak istiyorum**
	boono...yol-lamak istiyoRoom
– express _____	**Bunu acele posta servisi ile yollamak istiyorum**
	boonoo ahjeleh posta seRvisi ileh yol-lamak istiyoRoom
– by air mail _____	**Bunu uçak ile yollamak istiyorum**
	boonoo oochak ileh yol-lamak istiyoRoom
– by registered mail _____	**Bunu iadeli taahhütlü yollamak istiyorum**
	*boonoo i-**ah**deli **tah**-hewtlew yol-lamak istiyoRoom*

Telegram / fax

I'd like to send a _____ telegram to...	...telgraf çekmek istiyorum
	...telegRaf chekmek istiyoRoom
How much is that _____ per word?	Kelimesi kaç lira?
	kelimesi kach liRa?
This is the text I want ____ to send	Bu yollamak istediğim metin
	boo yol-lamak istedi:im metin
Shall I fill out the form ___ myself?	Formu kendim doldurayım mı?
	foRmoo kendim doldooRa-yuhm muh?
Can I make photocopies/ send a fax here?	Burada fotokopi/faks çekebilir miyim?
	booRada fotokopi/faks chekebiliR miyim?
How much is it _____ per page?	Sayfası kaç lira?
	sífasuh kach liRa?

9.2 Telephone

See also 1.8 Telephone alphabet

● **The PTTs have public phones** as well as postal facilities.
These may be better for international calls than the phone-booths in
the street. Public telephones do not take coins but tokens (jetons)
available from the PTT. Particularly for long-distance or international
calls, it is far easier to buy a phonecard (also from the PTT).
As in most countries, dial 00 44 for the UK, or 00 1 for the USA, then
miss out the initial zero from the area code.

Is there a phone box _____ around here?	Bu civarda bir telefon kulübesi var mı?
	boo jivaRda biR telefon koolewbesi vaR muh?
Could I use your _____ phone, please?	Telefonunuzu kullanabilir miyim?
	telefonoonoozoo kul-lanabiliR miyim?
Do you have a _____ (city/region)...phone directory?	Sizde (şehrinin/yöresinin)...telefon rehberi var mı?
	sizdeh (seHrinin/yurResinin)...telefon reHbeRi vaR muh?

Where can I get a _____ phone card?	**Nereden telefon kartı satın alabilirim?**
	neReden telefon kaRtuh satuhn alabiliRim?
Could you give me...? ___	**...verir misiniz?**
	...veRiR misiniz?
– the number for _____ international directory enquiries	**Bana yurt dışı istihbarat numarasını verir misiniz?**
	bana yooRt duhshuh istiHbaRat noomaRasuhnuh veRiR misiniz?
– the number of room... ___	**...numaralı odanın telefon numarasını verir misiniz?**
	...noomaRaluh odanuhn telefon noomaRasuhnuh veRiR misiniz?
– the international _____ access code	**Bana yurt dışı arama kodunu verir misiniz?**
	bana yooRt duhshshuh aRama kodoonoo veRiR misiniz?
– the country code for... ___	**...ülke kod numarasını verir misiniz?**
	...ewlkeh kod noomaRasuhnuh veRiR misiniz?
– the trunk code for... ___	**...şehir kod numarasını verir misiniz?**
	...shehiR kod noomaRasuhnuh veRiR misiniz?
– the number of... _____	**...telefon numarasını verir misiniz?**
	...telefon noomaRasuhnuh veRiR misiniz?
Could you check if this ___ number's correct?	**Bu numaranın doğru mu yanlış mı olduğunu soruşturabilir misiniz?**
	boo noomaRanuhn do:Roo moo yanluhsh muh oldoo:oonoo soRooshtooRabiliR misiniz?

Can I dial international direct?	**Yurt dışına otomatik olarak telefon açabilir miyim?**	
	yooRt duhshuhna otomatik olaRak telefon achabiliR miyim?	
Do I have to go through the switchboard?	**Santral aracılığı ile mi aramam gerek?**	
	santral aRajuhluh:uh ileh mi aRamam geRek?	
Do I have to dial '0' first?	**Önce sıfırı mı çevirmem gerekiyor?**	
	urnje suhfuhRuh muh cheviRmem geRekiyoR?	
Do I have to book my calls?	**Numarayı bağlatmam mı gerekiyor?**	
	noomaRa-yuh ba:latmam muh geRekiyoR?	
Could you dial this number for me, please?	**Benim için bu numarayı arar mısınız?**	
	benim ichin boo noomaRa-yuh aRaR muhsuhnuhz?	
Could you put me through to.../extension..., please?	**Beni...numara/... numaralı hat ile bağlayabilir misiniz?**	
	beni...noomaRa/...noomaRaluh hat ileh ba:la-yabiliR misiniz?	
I'd like to place a reverse-charge call to...	**...numarayı ödemeli olarak aramak istiyorum**	
	...noomaRa-yuh urdemeli olaRak aRamak istiyoRoom	
What's the charge per minute?	**Dakikası kaç lira?**	
	dakikasuh kach liRa?	
Have there been any calls for me?	**Beni arayan oldu mu?**	
	beni aRa-yan oldoo moo?	

The conversation

Hello, this is... _____	**İyi günler, ...ile görüşüyorsunuz**
	iyi gewnleR, ...ileh gurRewshew-yoRsoonooz
Who is this, please? _____	**Kiminle görüşüyorum?**
	kiminleh gurRewshew-yoRoom?
Is this...? _____	**... ile mi görüşüyorum?**
	... ileh mi gurRewshew-yoRoom?
I'm sorry, I've dialled ____	**Özür dilerim, yanlış numarayı çevirmişim**
the wrong number	*urzewR dileRim, yanluhsh noomaRa-yuh cheviRmishim*
I can't hear you _____	**Sizi duyamıyorum**
	sizi dooy-amuhyoRoom
I'd like to speak to..._____	**...ile görüşmek istiyorum**
	...ileh gurRewshmek istiyoRoom
Is there anybody _____	**İngilizce konuşmasını bilen biri var mı?**
who speaks English?	*ingilizjeh konooshmahsuhnuh bilen biRi vaR muh?*
Extension..., please _____	**...numaralı hattı bağlar mısınız?**
	...noomaRaluh hat-tuh ba:laR muhsuhnuhz?

Size telefon var	There's a phone call for you
Önce sıfırı çevirmeniz gerekiyor	You have to dial '0' first
Bir saniye lütfen	One moment, please
Cevap vermiyor	There's no answer
Telefon meşgul	The line's engaged
Lütfen bekleyiniz	Do you want to hold?
Sizi bağlıyorum	Putting you through
Elinizdeki numara yanlış	You've got a wrong number
Kendileri şu anda burada yok	He's/she's not here right now
Kendileri...kadar burada olacak	He'll/she'll be back...
Bu...telesekreteri	This is the answering machine of...

Could you ask him/her ___ to call me back?	**Beni aramasını söyler misiniz?**
	beni aRamasuhnuh suhyleR misiniz?
My name's... ___ My number's...	**Adım...Telefon numaram...**
	aduhm...telefon noomaRa ...
Could you tell him/her ___ I called?	**Aradığımı kendisine iletir misiniz?**
	aRaduh:uhmuh kendisineh iletiR misiniz?
I'll call back tomorrow ___	**Kendisini yarın tekrar ararım**
	kendisini yaRuhn tekRaR aRaRuhm

● **Opening times:** Shops are open from 9am to 7pm or even later.
Some shops (bakers and food shops) are open on Sunday mornings.

10.1 Shopping conversations

Where can I get...?	**Hangi dükkandan...satın alabilirim?**
	*hangi dewk-**kahn**-dan satuhn alabiliRim?*
When does this shop open?	**Bu dükkan saat kaçta açılıyor?**
	*boo dewk-**kahn** saht kachta achuhluhyoR?*
Could you tell me where the...department is?	**Bana...reyonunu gösterebilir misiniz?**
	bana...reyonoonoo gursterebiliR misiniz?
Could you help me, please? I'm looking for...	**Bana yardım edebilir misiniz?...arıyorum**
	bana yaRduhm edebiliR misiniz?...aRuhyoRoom
Do you sell English/ American newspapers?	**İngiliz ve Amerikan gazetesi satıyor musunuz?**
	ingilizj ve ameRikan gazetesi satuhyoR moosoonooz?

Size yardımcı olan var mı?　　Are you being served?

No, I'd like...	**Hayır...istiyordum**
	ha-yuhR...istiyoRdoom
I'm just looking, if that's all right	**Mahsuru yoksa sadece bakıyorum**
	maHsooRoo yoksa sadejeh bakuhyoRoom

Başka bir şey ister miydiniz?　　Anything else?

115

alış veriş merkezi shopping centre	**eczane** chemist	**mobilyacı** furniture shop
ayakkabı mağazası shoe shop	**elektrikli cihazlar** electrical appliances	**müzikçi** music shop
ayakkabı tamircisi cobbler	**fırın** bakery	**nalbur** hardware shop
baharatçı herbalist	**fotoğraf stüdyosu** photographer's studio	**oyuncakçı** toy shop
bakkal grocer's shop	**gazete bayii** newsagent's	**parfümeri** cosmetics and perfume shop/department
baklavacı baklava shop	**giyim mağazası** clothes shop	
balıkçı fishmonger	**gözlükçü** optician's	**pasaj** arcade
berber barber	**güzellik merkezi** beauty centre	**pastane** cake shop
bijuteri jeweller	**hediyelik eşya** gift shop	**pazar** market
bisiklet tamircisi cycle repair shop	**kapalı çarşı** covered market (in Istanbul Grand Bazaar)	**postane** post office
büfe free-standing kiosk selling newspapers, cigarettes, milk and cold drinks		**saat tamircisi** watch and clock repair shop
	kasap butchers	**şarküteri** delicatessen
butik boutique	**kırtasiye** stationery shop	**satış mağazası** direct factory sales outlet
çay bahçesi tea garden	**kitabevi** book shop	
çiçekçi florist	**kuaför** hairdresser's	**spor mağazası** sports shop
çömlekçi shop selling (earthenware) pots	**kürk mağazası** furriers	**süpermarket** supermarket
deri giyim mağazası leather-wear shop	**kuru temizleme** dry cleaners	**tekel** off-licence, wine shop
dondurmacı ice-cream seller	**manav** greengrocers	**terzi** tailor (either gents or ladies)
dükkan shop		

Yes, I'd also like... _____	**Evet, bana...verin** *evet...bana veRin*
No, thank you. That's all _	**Hayır, teşekkür ederim. Bu kadar** *ha-yuhr, teshek-kewR edeRim. boo kadaR*
Could you show me...? _	**Bana...gösterebilir misiniz?** *bana...gursteRebiliR misiniz?*
I'd prefer... _____	**...tercih ediyorum** *...teRji-h-ediyoRoom*
This is not what I'm _____ looking for	**Aradığım bu değil** *aRaduh:uhm boo de:il*
Thank you. I'll keep _____ looking	**Teşekkür ederim. Birkaç yere daha** **bakacağım** *teshek-kewR edeRim. biRkach yeReh da-ha* *bakaja:uhm*
Do you have_____ something...?	**Daha...bir şeyiniz yok mu?** *da-ha...biR sheyiniz yok moo?*
– less expensive? _____	**Daha ucuz bir şeyiniz yok mu?** *da-ha oojooz biR sheyiniz yok moo?*
– something smaller? ____	**Daha küçük bir şeyiniz yok mu?** *da-ha kewchewk biR sheyiniz yok moo?*
– something larger? _____	**Daha büyük bir şeyiniz yok mu?** *da-ha bew-yewk biR sheyiniz yok moo?*
I'll take this one_____	**Bunu alıyorum** *boonoo aluhyoRoom*

Kusura bakmayın, elimizde yok	I'm sorry, we don't have that
Kusura bakmayın, sonuncusu da **satıldı**	I'm sorry, we're sold out
Kusura bakmayın,...gelecek	I'm sorry, that won't be in until...
Kasaya ödeyiniz	You can pay at the cash desk
Kredi kartı kabul etmiyoruz	We don't accept credit cards
Seyahat çeki kabul etmiyoruz	We don't accept traveller's cheques
Döviz kabul etmiyoruz	We don't accept foreign currency

Does it come with _____ instructions?	**İçinde kullanma talimatı var mı?** *ichindeh kul-lanma talimatuh vaR muh?*
It's too expensive _____	**Çok pahalı** *chok pa-haluh*
I'll give you... _____	**...liraya verirseniz, alırım** *...liRa-ya veRiRseniz, aluhRuhm*
Could you keep this for __ me? I'll come back for it later	**Bunu benim için bir kenara ayırır mısınız? Biraz sonra gelir alırım** *boonoo benim ichin biR kenaRa a-yuhRuhR muhsuhnuhz? biRaz sonRa geliR aluhRuhm*
Have you got a bag _____ for me, please?	**Naylon torbanız var mı?** *nílon toRbanuhz vaR muh?*
Could you giftwrap _____ it, please?	**Hediyelik kağıda sarar mısınız?** *hediyelik ka:uhda saRaR muhsuhnuhz?*

10.2 Food

I'd like a hundred _____ grams of..., please	**Yüz gram...istiyorum** *yewz gRam...istiyoRoom*
– five hundred grams/ ___ half a kilo of...	**Yarım kilo...istiyorum** *yaRuhm kilo istiyoRoom*
– a kilo of..._____	**Bir kilo...istiyorum** *biR kilo...istiyoRoom*
Could you...it for me, ____ please?	**Bunu benim için...?** *boonoo benim ichin...?*
Could you slice it/ _____ dice it for me, please?	**Bunu benim için dilimler/keser misiniz?** *boonoo benim ichin dilimleR/keseR misiniz?*
Could you grate it _____ for me, please?	**Bunu benim için rendeler misiniz?** *boonoo benim ichin rendeleR misiniz?*
Can I order it? _____	**Ismarlıyabilir miyim?** *uhsmaRluhyabiliR miyim?*
I'll pick it up tomorrow/ __ at...	**Yarın/saat...gelir alırım** *yaRuhn/saht...geliR aluhRuhm*

Can you eat/drink this? _	**Bu yiyecek/içecek mi?**
	boo yiyejek/ichejek mi?
What's in it? _____	**İçinde ne var?**
	ichindeh neh vaR?

10.3 Clothing and shoes

I saw something in the___ window. Shall I point it out?	**Vitrinde bir şey gördüm. Göstereyim mi?** *vitRindeh biR shey gurRdewm. gursteReyim mi?*
I'd like something to_____ go with this	**Buna uyan bir şey istiyorum** *boona ooyan biR shey istiyoRoom*
Do you have shoes_____ to match this?	**Bu renk ayakkabınız var mı?** *boo renk a-yak-kabuhnuhz vaR muh?*
I'm a size...in the UK ____	**İngiltere'de...bedenim** *ingilteRedeh...bedenim*
Can I try this on? _____	**Bunu deneyebilir miyim?** *boonoo deneyebiliR miyim?*
Where's the fitting room?	**Kabin nerede?** *kabin neRedeh?*
It doesn't fit _____	**Olmadı** *olmaduh*
This is the right size _____	**Bu beden iyi** *boo beden iyi*
It doesn't suit me _____	**Yakışmadı** *yakuhshmaduh*
Do you have this/_____ these in...?	**Bunun...rengi var mı?** *boonoon...rengi vaR muh?*
The heel's too high/low __	**Topuğu çok yüksek/alçak** *topoo:oo chok yewksek/alchak*
Is this/are these_____ genuine leather?	**Bu/bunlar hakiki deri mi?** *boo/boonlaR hakiki deRi mi?*
I'm looking for a..._____ for a...-year-old baby/child	**...yaşındaki bebek/çocuk için...arıyorum** *...yashuhndahki bebek/chojook ichin...aRuhyoRoom*

ýtülemeyin Do not iron	**Islak asın** Drip dry	**Elde yıkayın** Hand wash
Sıkmayın Do not spin dry	**Kuru temizleme** Dry clean	**Makinede yıkanır** Machine wash

I'd like a... ... _____	**...bir...istiyorum** *biR...istiyoRoom*
– silk _____	**İpekten bir...istiyorum** *ipekten biR...istiyoRoom*
– cotton _____	**Pamuklu bir...istiyorum** *pamookloo bi ...istiyoRoom*
– woollen _____	**Yün bir...istiyorum** *yewn biR...istiyoRoom*
– linen _____	**Keten bir...istiyorum** *keten biR...istiyoRoom*

What temperature _____ can I wash it at?	**Bunu kaç derecede yıkayabilirim?** *boonoo kach deRejedeh yuhka-yabiliRim?*
Will it shrink in the _____ wash?	**Yıkandığında çeker mi?** *yuhkanduh:uhnda chekeR mi?*

At the cobbler's

Could you mend _____ these shoes?	**Bu ayakkabıları tamir edebilir misiniz?** *boo a-yak-kabuhlaRuh tahmiR edebiliR misiniz?*
Could you put new _____ soles/heels on these?	**Köseleyi/topukları yenileyebilir misiniz?** *kursheleyi/topooklaRuh yenileyebiliR misiniz?*
When will they be _____ ready?	**Ne zaman hazır olurlar?** *neh zaman hazuhR olooRlaR?*
I'd like..., please _____	**...istiyorum** *...istiyoRoom*

– a tin of shoe polish ____	**Bir kutu ayakkabı boyası istiyorum**
	biR kootoo ayuhk-kabuhsuh boyasuh istiyoRoom
– a pair of shoelaces ____	**Bir çift ayakkabı bağı istiyorum**
	biR chift ayak-kabuh ba:uh istiyoRoom

10.4 Photographs and video

I'd like a film for this ____ camera, please	**Bu makine için bir film istiyorum**
	boo makineh ichin biR film istiyoRoom
– a cartridge_____	**Bu makine için bir kaset film istiyorum**
	boo makineh ichin biR kaset film istiyoRoom
– a one twenty-six ____ cartridge	**Bu makine için yüz yirmi altılık bir kaset film istiyorum**
	boo makineh ichin yewz yiRmi altuhluhk biR kaset film istiyoRoom
– a slide film_____	**Bu makine için bir slayt istiyorum**
	boo makineh ichin biR slít istiyoRoom
– a film cartridge _____	**Bu makine için film kaseti istiyorum**
	boo makineh ichin film kaseti istiyoRoom
– a videotape_____	**Video kaseti istiyorum**
	video kaseti istiyoRoom
colour/black and white __	**renkli/siyah beyaz**
	renkli/siyaH beyaz
super eight_____	**süper sekiz**
	sewpeR sekiz
12/24/36 exposures ____	**on iki/yirmi dört/otuz altı pozluk**
	on iki/yiRmi durRt/otooz altuh pozlook
ASA/DIN number_____	**ASA/DIN sayısı**
	asa/din sa-yuhsuh
daylight film _____	**doğal ışık için film**
	do:al uhshuhk ichin film
film for artificial light ____	**yapay ışık için film**
	yapí uhshuhk ichin film

Problems

Could you load the _____ film for me, please?	**Filmi makineye takar mısınız?** *filmi makineyeh takaR muhsuhnuhz?*
Could you take the film __ out for me, please?	**Filmi makineden çıkarır mısınız?** *filmi makineden chuhkaRuhR muhsuhnuhz?*
Should I replace _____ the batteries?	**Pilleri değiştirmem gerekir mi?** *pil-leRi de:ishtiRmem geRekiR mi?*
Could you have a look ___ at my camera, please? It's not working	**Makineme bir bakar mısınız? Çalışmıyor** *makinemeh biR bakaR muhsuhnuhz? chaluhshmuhyoR*
The...is broken_____	**...bozuk** *...bozook*
The film's jammed_____	**Film takılmış** *film takuhlmuhsh*
The film's broken_____	**Film yırtılmış** *film yuhRtuhlmuhsh*
The flash isn't working ___	**Flaş çalışmıyor** *flash chaluhshmuhyoR*

Processing and prints

I'd like to have this film __ developed/printed, please	**Bu filmi banyo ettirmek/bastırmak istiyorum** *boo filmi banyo et-tiRmek/bastuhRmak istiyoRoom*
I'd like...prints from_____ each negative	**Her negatiften...baskı istiyorum** *heR negatiften...baskuh istiyoRoom*
glossy/mat _____	**parlak/mat** *paRlak/mat*
6x9_____	**altı çarpı dokuz** *altuh chaRpuh dokooz*
I'd like to re-order _____ these photos	**Bu fotoğrafları çoğalttırmak istiyorum** *boo foto:Raflaruh cho:alt-tuhRmak istiyoRoom*

I'd like to have this _____ photo enlarged	**Bu fotoğrafı büyüttürmek istiyorum** *boo foto:Rafuh bew-yewt-tewRmek istiyoRoom*
How much is _____ processing?	**Banyo ettirmek ne kadar tutar?** *banyo et-tiRmek neh kadaR tootaR?*
– printing_____	**Fotoğrafları bastırmak ne kadar tutar?** *foto:RaflaRuh bastuhRmak neh kadaR tootaR?*
– it to re-order _____	**Fotoğrafları çoğalttırmak ne kadar tutar?** *foto:RaflaRuh cho:alt-tuhRmak neh kadaR tootaR?*
– the enlargement_____	**Fotoğrafları büyüttürmek ne kadar tutar?** *foto:RaflaRuh bew-yewt-tewRmek neh kadaR tootaR?*

10.5 At the hairdresser's

When will they _____ be ready?	**Ne zaman hazır olurlar?** *neh zaman hazuhR olooRlaR?*
Do I have to make an____ appointment?	**Randevu almam gerekiyor mu?** *randevoo almam geRekiyoR moo?*
Can I come in straight ___ away?	**Bana şimdi yardımcı olabilir misiniz?** *bana shimdi yaRduhmjuh olabiliR misiniz?*
How long will I have _____ to wait?	**Ne kadar beklemem gerekiyor?** *neh kadaR beklemem geRekiyoR?*
I'd like a shampoo/_____ haircut	**Saçımı yıkatmak/kestirmek istiyorum** *sachumuh yuhkatmak/kestiRmek istiyoRoom*
I'd like a shampoo for ___ oily/dry hair, please	**Yağlı/kuru saç için şampuan istiyorum** *ya:luh/kooRoo sach ichin shampooan istiyoRoom*
– an anti-dandruff _____ shampoo	**Kepekli saç için şampuan istiyorum** *kepekli sach ichin shampooan istiyoRoom*

– a shampoo for _____ permed/coloured hair	**Permalı saç/boyalı saç için şampuan istiyorum**
	peRmaluh sach/boy-aluh sach ichin shampooan istiyoRoom
– a colour rinse shampoo	**Boyalı şampuan istiyorum**
	boy-aluh shampooan istiyoRoom
– a shampoo with _____ conditioner	**Kremli şampuan istiyorum**
	kRemli shampooan istiyoRoom
– highlights _____	**Saçlarıma röfle yaptırmak istiyorum**
	sachlaRuhma rurfleh yaptuhRmak istiyoRoom
Do you have a colour ____ chart, please?	**Renk kataloğunuz var mı?**
	renk katalo:oonooz vaR muh?
I want to keep it the _____ same colour	**Saçımın aynı renk kalmasını istiyorum**
	sachuhmuhn ínuh renk kalmasuhnuh istiyoRoom
I'd like it darker/lighter ___	**Saçımın daha koyu/açık olmasını istiyorum**
	sachuhmuh da-ha koyoo/achuhk olmasuhnuh istiyoRoom
I'd like/I don't want _____ hairspray	**Saç spreyi istiyorum (istemiyorum)**
	sach spreyi istiyoRoom (istemiyoRoom)
– gel _____	**Saçıma jöle sürmenizi istiyorum (istemiyorum)**
	sachuhma zhurleh sewRmenizi istiyoRoom (istemiyoRoom)
– lotion _____	**Saçıma losyon sürmenizi istiyorum (istemiyorum)**
	sachuhma losyon sewRmenizi istiyoRoom (istemiyoRoom)
I'd like a short fringe_____	**Kakülümün kısa olmasını istiyorum**
	kahkewlewmewn kuhsa olmasuhnuh istiyoRoom
Not too short at the back	**Saçımın arkasından çok almayın**
	sachuhmuhn aRkasuhndan chok alma-yuhn

Not too long here _____	**Burasını çok uzun bırakmayın** *booRasuhnuh chok oozoon buhRakma-* *yuhn*
I'd like/I don't want _____ (many) curls	**(çok) dalgalı olsun (olmasın)** *(chok) dalgaluh olsoon (olmasuhn)*
It needs a little/ _____ a lot taken off	**Saçımın çok az/saçımın kısa kesilmesi** **gerek** *sachuhmuhn chok az/sachuhmuhn kuhsa* *kesilmesi geRek*
I want a completely _____ different style	**Değişik bir model istiyorum** *de:ishik biR model istiyoRoom*
I'd like it the same... _____	**Saçımın...gibi olmasını istiyorum** *sachuhmuhn...gibi olmasuhnuh* *istiyoRoom*
– as that lady's _____	**Saçımın o bayanınki gibi olmasını** **istiyorum** *sachuhmuhn o ba-yanuhnki gibi* *olmasuhnuh istiyoRoom*
– as in this photo _____	**Saçımın bu resimdeki gibi olmasını** **istiyorum** *sachuhmuhn boo resimdeki gibi* *olmasuhnuh istiyoRoom*
Could you put the _____ drier up/down a bit?	**Saç kurutma makinesini açar/kısar mısınız?** *sach kooRootma makinesini achaR/kuhsaR* *muhsuhnuhz?*
I'd like a facial _____	**Yüzüme temizleyici maske yaptırmak** **istiyorum** *yewzewme temizleyiji maskeh yaptuhRmak* *istiyoRoom*
– a manicure _____	**Manikür yaptırmak istiyorum** *manikewR yaptuhRmak istiyoRoom*
– a massage _____	**Masaj yaptırmak istiyorum** *masazh yaptuhRmak istiyoRoom*

Could you trim _____ my fringe?	**Kakülümün ucundan alır mısınız?** *kakewlewmewn oojoondan aluhR muhsuhnuhz?*
– my beard? _____	**Sakalımın ucundan alır mısınız?** *sakaluhmuhn oojoondan aluhR muhsuhnuhz?*
– my moustache? _____	**Bıyığımın ucundan alır mısınız?** *buhyuhmuhn oojoondan aluhR muhsuhnuhz?*
I'd like a shave, please __	**Sakal tıraşı lütfen** *sakal tuhRashuh lewtfen*
I'd like a wet shave, _____ please	**Tıraş olmak istiyorum** *tuhRash olmak istiyoRoom*

Saçınızın nasıl kesilmesini isterdiniz?	How do you want it cut?
Hangi modeli isterdiniz?	What style did you have in mind?
Saçınızın hangi renge boyanmasını isterdiniz?	What colour do you want it?
Bu sıcaklık iyi mi?	Is the temperature all right for you?
Okuyacak bir şey ister misiniz?	Would you like something to read?
Bir şey içer misiniz?	Would you like a drink?
Nasıl, beğendiniz mi?	Is this what you had in mind?

11

At the Tourist Information Centre

11.1 Places of interest

Where's the Tourist _____ Information, please?	**Danışma bürosu nerede?** *danuhshma bewRosoo neRedeh?*
Do you have a city map?_	**Sizde şehrin haritası var mı?** *sizdeh sheHrin haRitasuh vaR muh?*
Could you give me _____ some information about...?	**Bana...hakkında bilgi verebilir misiniz?** *bana...hak-kuhnda bilgi veRebiliR misiniz?*
How much is that? _____	**Borcum ne kadar?** *boRjum neh kadaR?*
What are the main_____ places of interest?	**Görülmeye değer ne var?** *gurRewlmeyeh de:eR neh vaR?*
Could you point them ___ out on the map?	**Haritada gösterebilir misiniz?** *haRitada gursteRebiliR misiniz?*
What do you _____ recommend?	**Ne tavsiye edersiniz?** *neh tavsiyeh edeRsiniz?*
We'll be here for a_____ few hours	**Burada birkaç saat kalacağız** *booRada biRkach saht kalaja:uhz*
– a day _____	**Burada bir gün kalacağız** *booRada biR gewn kalaja:uhz*
– a week _____	**Burada bir hafta kalacağız** *booRada biR hafta kalaja:uhz*
We're interested in..._____	**...ilgimizi çekiyor** *...ilgimizi chekiyoR*
Is there a scenic walk_____ around the city?	**Şehirde gezinti yapmak için güzel yerler var mı?** *sheHiRdeh gezinti yapmak ichin gewzel yeRleR vaR muh?*
How long does it take? __	**Ne kadar sürer?** *neh kadaR sewReR?*
Where does it start/end?_	**Başlangıç/bitiş noktası nerede?** *bashlan-guhch/bitish noktasuh neRedeh?*
Are there any boat _____ cruises here?	**Burada gezi vapurları var mi?** *booRada gezi vapooRlaRuh vaR muh?*

Where can we board?	**Nereden binebiliriz?**
	neReden binebiliRiz?
Are there any bus tours?	**Otobüsle gezi turu var mı?**
	otobewsleh gezi tooRoo vaR muh?
Where do we get on?	**Nereden binebiliriz?**
	neReden binebiliRiz?
Is there a guide who speaks English?	**İngilizce konuşmasını bilen bir rehber var mı?**
	ingilizjeh konooshmasuhnuh bilen biR reHbeR vaR muh?
What trips can we take around the area?	**Çevrede ne gibi gezintiler yapmak mümkün?**
	chevRedeh neh gibi gezintileR yapmak mewmkewn?
Are there any excursions?	**Turistik geziler var mı?**
	tooRistik gezileR vaR muh?
Where do they go to?	**Nereye gezi var?**
	neReyeh gezi vaR?
We'd like to go to...	**... gitmek istiyoruz**
	... gitmek istiyoRooz
How long is the trip?	**Gezi ne kadar sürer?**
	gezi neh kadaR sewReR?
How long do we stay in...?	**...ne kadar kalacağız?**
	...neh kadaR kalaja:uhz?
Are there any guided tours?	**Rehber eşliğinde gezileriniz var mı?**
	reHbeR eshli:indeh gezileRiniz vaR muh?
How much free time will we have there?	**Gezmek için ne kadar zamanımız var?**
	gezmek ichin neh kadaR zamanuhmuhz vaR?
We want to go hiking	**Hiking yapmak istiyoruz**
	híking yapmak istiyoRooz
Can we hire a guide?	**Bir rehber kiralayabilir miyiz?**
	biR reHbeR kiRala-yabiliR miyiz?
Can I book mountain huts?	**Dağ kulübesi ayırtabilir miyim?**
	da: koolewbesi a-yuhRtabiliR miyim?
What time does... open/close?	**...saat kaçta açılıyor/kapanıyor?**
	...saht kachta achuhluhyoR/kapanuhyoR

What days is...open/ closed?	...haftanın hangi günleri açık/kapalı?
	...haftanuhn hangi gewnleRi achuhk/kapaluh?
What's the admission price?	Giriş ücreti ne kadar?
	giRish ewchReti neh kadaR?
Is there a group discount?	Gurup indirimi yapıyor musunuz?
	gooRoop indiRimi yapuhyoR moosoonooz?
Is there a child discount?	Çocuklara indirim var mı?
	chojooklaRa indiRim vaR muh?
Is there a discount for pensioners?	Emeklilere indiriminiz var mı?
	emeklileReh indiRiminiz vaR muh?
Can I take (flash) photos/can I film here?	Burada (flaşla) fotoğraf/film çekebilir miyim?
	booRada (flashla) foto:Raf/film chekebiliR miyim?
Do you have any postcards of...?	üzerinde...olan kartpostal satıyor musunuz?
	ewzeRindeh...olan kaRtpostal satuhyoR moosoonooz?
Do you have an English...?	İngilizce bir...var mı?
	ingilizjeh biR...vaR muh?
– an English catalogue?	İngilizce bir kataloğunuz var mı?
	ingilizjeh biR katalo:oonooz vaR muh?
– an English programme?	İngilizce bir programınız var mı?
	ingilizjeh biR pRogRamuhnuhz vaR muh?
– an English brochure?	İngilizce bir broşürünüz var mı?
	ingilizjeh biR bRoshewRewnewz vaR muh?

11.2 Going out

● **In Turkish theatres,** you will be shown to your seat by an attendant who will also (usually) give you a free leaflet about the play. You should offer a tip (maybe 5 or 10 percent of the ticket price) Most films are dubbed into Turkish (*Türkçe seslendirilmiş*) but those which are subtitled will be advertised as *alt yazılı* or *orijinali*.

Do you have this _____ week's/month's entertainment guide?	**Sizde bu haftanın/ayın etkinlik dergisi var mı?** *sizdeh boo haftanuhn/i-uhn etkinlik deRgisi vaR muh?*
What's on tonight? _____	**Bu akşam yapılacak ne var?** *boo aksham yapuhlajak neh vaR?*
We want to go to... _____	**...gitmek istiyoruz** *...gitmek istiyoRooz*
Which films are _____ showing?	**Hangi filmler gösteriliyor?** *hangi filmleR gursteRiliyoR?*
What sort of film is that? _	**Nasıl bir film?** *nasuhl biR film?*
Suitable for the whole ___ family	**her yaş için** *heR yash ichin*
not suitable for _____ children under 16 years	**16 yaşından küçükler giremez** *16 yashuhndan kewchewkleR giRemez*
original version _____	**orijinali** *orizhinali*
subtitled _____	**alt yazılı** *alt yazuhluh*
dubbed _____	**Türkçe seslendirilmiş** *tewRkcheh seslendiRilmish*
Is it a continuous_____ showing?	**Gösteri aralıksız mı?** *gursteRi aRaluhksuhz muh?*
What's on at...? _____	**...ne var?** *...neh vaR?*
– the theatre?_____	**Tiyatroda ne var?** *tiyatRoda neh vaR?*

– the concert hall? _____	**Konser merkezinde ne var?**
	konseR meRkezindeh neh vaR?
– the opera? _____	**Operada ne var?**
	opeRada neh vaR?
Where can I find a good _ disco around here?	**Bu civarda nerede iyi bir diskotek var?**
	boo jivaRda neRedeh iyi biR diskotek vaR?
Is it members only? _____	**Üye olmak şart mı?**
	ewyeh olmak shaRt muh?
Where can I find a good _ nightclub around here?	**Bu civarda nerede iyi bir gece kulübü var?**
	boo jivaRda neRedeh iyi biR gejeh koolewbew vaR?
Is it evening wear only? __	**Gece kıyafeti şart mı?**
	gejeh kuhyafeti shaRt muh?

Hangi gösteri için yer ayırtmak istiyorsunuz?	Which performance do you want to book for?
Ne tarafta oturmak isterdiniz?	Where would you like to sit?
Bilet kalmadı	Everything's sold out
Sadece ayakta yer var	It's standing room only
Sadece balkonda yer var	We've only got balcony seats left
Sadece galeride yer var	We've only got seats left in the gallery
Sadece salonda yer var	We've only got stalls seats left
Sadece ön tarafta yer var	We've only got seats left at the front
Sadece arka tarafta yer var	We've only got seats left at the back
Kaç bilet istiyorsunuz?	How many seats would you like?
Biletleri saat...önce almanız gerekiyor	You'll have to pick up the tickets before...o'clock
Biletinizi görebilir miyim?	Tickets, please
Yeriniz burası	This is your seat
Yanlış yerde oturuyorsunuz	You're in the wrong seats

Should I/we dress up? ___	**Gece kıyafeti isteniyor mu?**
	gejeh kuhyafeti isteniyoR moo?
What time does the _____ show start?	**Gösteri saat kaçta başlıyor?**
	gursteRi saht kachta bashluhyoR?
When's the next soccer ___ match?	**Bir sonraki futbol maçı ne zaman?**
	biR sonRaki footbol machuh neh zaman?
Who's playing? _____	**Maç hangi takımlar arasında?**
	mach hangi takuhmlaR aRasuhnda?

11.3 Booking tickets

Could you book some ___ tickets for us?	**Bizim için yer ayırabilir misiniz?**
	bizim ichin yeR a-yuhRabiliR misiniz?
We'd like to book..._____ seats/a table...	**...yer/bir masa istiyoruz**
	...yeR/biR masa istiyoRooz
– in the stalls _____	**Salonda...yer/bir masa istiyoruz**
	salonda...yeR/biR masa istiyoRooz
– on the balcony _____	**Balkonda...yer/bir masa istiyoruz**
	balkonda...yeR/biR masa istiyoRooz
– box seats_____	**Locada...yer istiyoruz**
	lojada...yeR istiyoRooz
– a table at the front _____	**Ön tarafta...bir masa istiyoruz**
	urn taRafta...biR masa istiyoRooz
– in the middle_____	**Ortada...bir masa istiyoruz**
	oRtada...biR masa istiyoRooz
– at the back _____	**Arka tarafta...bir masa istiyoruz**
	aRka taRafta...biR masa istiyoRooz
Could I book...seats for ___ the...o'clock performance?	**Saat...gösteri için...bilet ayırtabilir miyim?**
	saht...gursteRi ichin...bilet a-yuhRtabiliR miyim?
Are there any seats left ___ for tonight?	**Bu akşamki gösteri için biletiniz var mı?**
	boo akshamki gursteRi ichin biletiniz vaR muh?
How much is a ticket? ___	**Bir biletin fiyatı ne kadar?**
	biR biletin fiyatuh neh kadaR?

When can I pick the _____
tickets up?

Biletleri saat kaçta gelip alabilirim?
biletleRi saht kachta gelip alabiliRim?

I've got a reservation _____

Yer ayırtmıştım
yeR a-yuhRtmuhshtuhm

My name's..._____

Adım...
aduhm...

12.1 Sporting questions

Where can we... _____ around here?	**Burada nerede...?** *booRada neRedeh...?*
Is there a... _____ around here?	**Bu civarda bir...var mı?** *boo jivaRda biR...vaR muh?*
Can I hire a...here? _____	**Burada bir...kiralayabilir miyim?** *booRada biR...kiRala-yabiliR miyim?*
Can I take...lessons? ____	**...dersi alabilir miyim?** *...deRsi alabiliR miyim?*
How much is that per____ hour/per day/a turn?	**Saati/günlüğü/bir kereliği ne kadar?** *sahti/gewnlew:ew/biR keReli:i neh kadaR?*
Do I need a permit _____ for that?	**Ruhsat gerekli mi?** *ruHsat geRekli mi?*
Where can I get_____ the permit?	**Bu ruhsatı nereden alabilirim?** *boo ruHsat neReden alabiliRim?*

12.2 By the waterfront

Is it a long way to _____ the sea still?	**Denize daha çok uzak mı?** *denizeh da-ha chok oozak muh?*
Is there a...around here? _	**Bu civarda bir...var mı?** *boo jivaRda biR...vaR muh?*
– an outdoor/indoor/ _____ public swimming pool	**Bu civarda bir yüzme havuzu var mı?** *boo jivaRda biR yewzmeh havoozoo vaR muh?*
– a sandy beach _____	**Bu civarda bir kumsal var mı?** *boo jivaRda biR koomsal vaR muh?*
– a nudist beach _____	**Bu civarda bir çıplaklar plajı var mı?** *boo jivaRda biR chuhplaklaR plazhuh vaR muh?*
– mooring _____	**Bu civarda bir yat limanı var mı?** *boo jivaRda biR yat limanuh vaR muh?*

Are there any rocks here?	**Burası kayalık mı?** *booRasuh ka-yaluhk da vaR muh?*
When's high/low tide?	**Deniz ne zaman kabarıyor/alçalıyor?** *deniz neh zaman kabaRuhyoR/alchaluhyoR?*
What's the water temperature?	**Su kaç derece?** *soo kach deRejeh?*
Is it (very) deep here?	**Burası (çok) derin mi?** *booRasuh (chok) deRin mi?*
Can you stand here?	**Burada ayakta durulabilir mi?** *booRada a-yakta dooRoolabiliR mi?*
Is it safe to swim here?	**Burada yüzmek (çocuklar için) tehlikeli değil mi?** *booRada yewzmek (chojooklaR ichin) teHlikeli de:il mi?*
Are there any currents?	**Akıntı var mı?** *akuhntuh vaR muh?*
Are there any rapids/ waterfalls in this river?	**Bu nehrin hızlı akıntı yeri/şelalesi var mı?** *boo neHRin huhzluh akuhntuhluh yeRi/shelalesi vaR muh?*
What does that flag/ buoy mean?	**O bayrak/şamandıra ne anlamına geliyor?** *o bírak/shamanduhRa neh anlamuhna geliyoR?*
Is there a life guard on duty here?	**Burada bir cankurtaran var mı?** *booRada biR jankooRtaRan vaR muh?*
Are dogs allowed here?	**Köpeklerin girmesi yasak mı?** *kurpekleRin giRmesi yasak muh?*
Is camping on the beach allowed?	**Plajda kamp kurmak yasak mı?** *plazhda kamp kooRmak yasak muh?*
Are we allowed to build a fire here?	**Burada ateş yakmak yasak mı?** *booRada atesh yakmak yasak muh?*

Balık tutmak yasaktır No fishing	Sadece ruhsat ile Only with a permit	**Tehlike** Danger
Balık tutulur Fishing water	**Sörf yapmak yasaktır** No surfing	**Yüzmek yasaktır** No swimming

12.3 In the snow

Can I take ski lessons ___ here?	**Burada kayak dersi alabilir miyim?** *booRada ka-yak deRsi alabiliR miyim?*
for beginners/advanced ___	**Yeni başlayanlar/(biraz) ilerlemiş olanlar** *yeni bashla-yanlaR/(biRaz) ileRlemish olanlaR*
How large are the _____ groups?	**Guruplar kaç kişilik?** *gooRooplaR kach kishilik?*
What language are _____ the classes in?	**Dersler hangi dilde veriliyor?** *deRsleR hangi dildeh veRiliyoR?*
I'd like a lift pass, _____ please	**Bir kayak (telesiyej/teleferik) pasosu istiyorum** *biR ka-yak (telesiyezh/telefeRik) pasosoo istiyoRoom*
Must I give you a _____ passport photo?	**Vesikalık fotoğraf gerekir.** *vesikaluhk foto:Raf geRekiR*
Where can I have a_____ passport photo taken?	**Nerede vesikalık fotoğraf çektirebilirim?** *neRedeh vesikaluhk foto:raf chektiRebiliRim?*
Where are the _____ beginners' slopes?	**Yeni başlayanlar için kayak pisti nerede?** *yeni bashla-yanlaR ichin ka-yak pisti neRedeh?*
Are the...in operation? ___	**...açık mı?** *...achuhk muh?*
– the ski lifts_____	**Teleferik açık mı?** *telefeRik achuhk muh?*
– the chair lifts_____	**Telesiyej açık mı?** *telesiyezh achuhk muh?*

13.1 Call (fetch) the doctor

Could you call/fetch a ___ doctor quickly, please?	**Hemen bir doktor çağırır mısınız lütfen?** *hemen biR dokoR cha:uhRuhR muhsuhnuhz lewtfen?*
When does the doctor ___ have surgery?	**Doktorun görüşme saatleri ne zaman?** *doktoRoon gurRewshmeh sahtleRi neh zaman?*
When can the doctor ___ come?	**Doktor ne zaman gelebilir?** *doktoR neh zaman geliR?*
I'd like to make an ___ appointment to see the doctor	**Benim için doktordan bir randevu alabilir misiniz?** *benim ichin doktoRdan biR randevoo alabiliR misiniz?*
I've got an appointment ___ to see the doctor at...	**Saat...doktorla randevum var** *saht...doktoRla randevoom vaR*
Which doctor/chemist ___ has night/weekend duty?	**Hangi doktorun/eczanenin gece/hafta sonu nöbeti var?** *hangi doktoRoon/ejzanenin gejeh/hafta sonoo nurbeti vaR?*

13.2 Patient's ailments

I don't feel well ___	**Kendimi iyi hissetmiyorum** *kendimi iyi his-setmiyoRoom*
I'm dizzy ___	**Başım dönüyor** *bashuhm durnew-yoR*
– ill ___	**Hastayım** *hasta-yuhm*
– sick ___	**Midem bulanıyor** *midem boolanuhyoR*
I've got a cold ___	**Nezleyim** *nezleyim*

It hurts here _____	**Buram ağrıyor**
	booRam a:RuhyoR
I've been throwing up ___	**İstifrağ ettim**
	istifra: et-tim
I've got..._____	**...şikayetçiyim**
	...shika-yet-chiyim
I'm running a _____ temperature of...degrees	**Ateşim...derece** *ateshim...deRejeh*
I've been stung by _____ a wasp	**Beni eşek arısı soktu** *beni eshek aRuhsuh soktoo*
I've been stung by an___ insect	**Beni böcek ısırdı** *beni burjek uhsuhRduh*
I've been bitten by _____ a dog	**Beni köpek ısırdı** *beni kurpek uhsuhRduh*
I've been stung by _____ a jellyfish	**Bana deniz anası değdi** *bana deniz anasuh de:di*
I've been bitten by _____ a snake	**Beni yılan ısırdı** *beni yuhlan uhsuhRduh*
I've been bitten by _____ an animal	**Beni bir hayvan ısırdı** *beni biR hívan uhsuhRduh*
I've cut myself _____	**kendimi kestim** *kendimi kestim*
I've burned myself _____	**kendimi yaktım** *kendimi yaktuhm*
I've grazed myself_____	**kendimi yüzdüm** *kendimi yewzdewm*
I've had a fall _____	**Düştüm** *dewshtewm*
I've sprained my ankle ___	**Ayak bileğimi burktum** *a-yak bile:imi booRktoom*
I've come for the pil	**Doğum kontrol hapı istiyorum, lütfen** *do:oom kontRol hapuh istiyoRoom, lewtfen*

13.3 The consultation

Şikayetiniz nedir?	What seems to be the problem?
Bu şikayetleriniz başlayalı ne kadar oluyor?	How long have you had these symptoms?
Bu şikayetleriniz geçmişte de var mıydı?	Have you had this trouble before?
Ateşiniz kaç derece?	How high is your temperature?
Lütfen, soyununuz	Get undressed, please
Belden yukarsını çıkarın	Strip to the waist, please
Şurada soyunabilirsiniz	You can undress there
Sağ/sol kolunuzu sıvar mısınız?	Roll up your left/right sleeve, please
Buraya uzanın	Lie down here, please
Acıyor mu?	Does this hurt?
Derin nefes alıp verin	Breathe deeply
Ağzınızı açın	Open your mouth

Patient's medical history

I'm a diabetic _____	**Şeker hastasıyım** *shekeR hastasuhyuhm*
I have a heart condition __	**Kalp hastasıyım** *kalp hastasuhyuhm*
I have asthma _____	**Astım hastasıyım** *astuhm hastasuhyuhm*
I'm allergic to... _____	**...karşı alerjim var** *...kaRshuh aleRzhim vaR*
I'm...months pregnant __	**...aylık hamileyim** *...íluhk hahmileyim*
I'm on a diet _____	**Perhizdeyim** *peRhizdeyim*

Herhangi bir şeye karşı alerjiniz var mı?	Do you have any allergies?
İlaç kullanıyor musunuz?	Are you on any medication?
Perhizde misiniz?	Are you on a diet?
Hamile misiniz?	Are you pregnant?
Tetanoz aşısı oldunuz mu?	Have you had a tetanus injection?

I'm on medication/the pill	**İlaç/doğum kontrol hapı kullanıyorum**
	ilach/do:oom kontRol hapuh kul-lanuhyoRoom
I've had a heart attack ___ once before	**Daha önce de kalp krizi geçirdim**
	da-ha urnjeh deh kalp kRizi gechiRdim
I've had a(n)...operation __	**...ameliyat oldum**
	...ameliyat oldoom
I've been ill recently _____	**Bir müddet önce hastaydım**
	biR mewd-det urnjeh hastíduhm

The diagnosis

I've got an ulcer _____	**Ülserim var**
	ewlseRim vaR
I've got my period_____	**Adet kanamam başladı**
	adet kanamam bashladuh
Is it contagious? _____	**Bulaşıcı mı?**
	boolashuhjuh muh
How long do I have to ___ stay...?	**... ne kadar kalmam gerek?**
	... neh kadaR kalmam geRek?
– in bed_____	**Yatakta ne kadar kalmam gerek?**
	yatakta neh kadaR kalmam geRek?
– in hospital _____	**Hastanede ne kadar kalmam gerek?**
	hastanedeh neh kadaR kalmam geRek?
Do I have to go on _____ a special diet?	**Perhiz yapmak zorunda mıyım?**
	peRhiz yapmak zoRoonda muhyuhm?

Pek bir şeyiniz yok	It's nothing serious
...kırmışsınız	Your...is broken
...berelenmişsiniz	You've got a/some bruised...
...kopmuş	You've got (a) torn...
İltihaplanma var	You've got an inflammation
Apandisitiniz var	You've got appendicitis
Bronşitiniz var	You've got bronchitis
Cinsel bir hastalığa yakalanmışsınız	You've got a venereal disease
Gripe yakalanmışsınız	You've got the flu
Kalp krizi geçirmişsiniz	You've had a heart
Mikrop kapmışsınız	attack
Zatürree olmuşsunuz	You've got an infection (viral,
Ülseriniz var	bacterial)
Kasınızı zorlayıp incitmişsiniz	You've got pneumonia
Vajinal enfeksiyonunuz var	You've got an ulcer
Yediğiniz gıdadan zehirlenmişsiniz	You've pulled a muscle
Sizi güneş çarpmış	You've got a vaginal infection
... karşı alerjiniz var	You've got food poisoning
Hamilesiniz	You've got sunstroke
Kanınızı/idrarınızı/dışkınızı araştırtmak istiyorum	You're allergic to... You're pregnant I'd like to have your
Dikiş atılması gerek	blood/urine/stools tested
Sizi bir uzman doktora/hastaneye gönderiyorum	It needs stitching I'm referring you to a specialist/sending you to hospital
Röntgen fotoğraflarının çekilmesi gerek	You'll need to have some x-rays taken
Bir süre daha bekleme odasında oturmanız gerek	Could you wait in the waiting room, please?
Ameliyat olmanız gerek	You'll need an operation

Am I allowed to travel? __	**Seyahat edebilir miyim?**	
	seyahat edebiliR miyim?	
Can I make a new_____ appointment?	**Yeni bir randevu alabilir miyim?**	
	yeni biR randevoo alabiliR miyim?	
When do I have to _____ come back?	**Tekrar ne zaman gelmem gerek?**	
	tekRaR neh zaman gelmem geRek?	
I'll come back _____ tomorrow	**Yarın tekrar gelirim**	
	yaRuhn tekRaR geliRim	

Yarın/...gün sonra yeniden gelmelisiniz	Come back tomorrow/in...days' time

13.4 Medication and prescriptions

bu ilaçarı aldıktan sonra araba kullanmayınız	**kapsül** capsules	**tedaviyi tamamlayın** finish the course
do not drive after taking this medicine	**merhem** ointment	**tümünü yutun** swallow whole
damla drops	**...saatte bir** every...hours	**yemeklerden önce** before meals
...gün boyunca throughout the day	**sadece dıştan kullanılır** not for internal use	**(yemek/çay) kaşığı** spoonfuls (tablespoons/ teaspoons)
günde...kere ...times a day	**sürün** rub on	**yutun** swallow
iğne injections	**suyla karıştırın** dissolve in water	
	tablet tablets	

Size antibiyotik/şurup/ sakinleştirici/ağrı kesici yazıyorum	I'm prescribing antibiotics/a mixture/a tranquillizer/pain killers
Dinlenmelisiniz	Have lots of rest
Dışarı çıkmamalısınız	Stay indoors
Yatakta kalmalısınız	Stay in bed

How do I take this_____ medicine?

Bu ilaçları nasıl almam gerekiyor?

boo ilachlaR nasuhl almam geRekiyoR?

How many capsules/ ____ drops/injections/ spoonfuls/tablets each time?

Her seferinde kaç kapsül/damla/iğne/kaşık/tablet?

heR sefeRindeh kach kapsewl/damla/i:neh/kashuhk/tablet?

How many times a day? _

Günde kaç defa?

gewndeh kach defa?

I've forgotten my _____ medication. At home I take...

İlaçlarımı unutmuşum. İngiltere'de...kullanıyorum

ilachlaRuhm oonootmooshoom. ingilteRedeh...kool-lanuhyoRoom

Could you make out a ___ prescription for me?

Bana bir reçete verebilir misiniz?

bana biR recheteh veRebiliR misiniz?

13.5 At the dentist's

Do you know a good _____ dentist?	**Bana iyi bir diş doktoru tavsiye edebilir misiniz?**
	bana iyi biR dish doktoRoo tavsiyeh edebiliR misiniz?
Could you make a_____ dentist's appointment for me? It's urgent	**Benim için diş doktorundan randevu alabilir misiniz? Acelem var**
	benim ichin dish doktooRoondan randevoo alabiliR misiniz? ajelem vaR
Can I come in today, _____ please?	**Bugün gelebilir miyim lütfen?**
	boogewn gelebiliR miyim lewtfen?
I have (terrible)_____ toothache	**Dişim (felaket) ağrıyor**
	dishim (felahket) a:RiyoR
Could you prescribe/ _____ give me a painkiller?	**Ağrı kesici yazabilir mısınız/verebilir misiniz?**
	a:Ruh kesiji yazabiliR misiniz?/veRebiliR misiniz?
A piece of my tooth _____ has broken off	**Dişimin bir parçası kırıldı**
	dishimin biR paRchasuh kuhRuhlduh

Hangi dişiniz ağrıyor?	Which tooth hurts?
Abseniz var	You've got an abscess
Kanal tedavisi yapmam gerekiyor	I'll have to do a root canal
Lokal anestezi yapacağüm	I'm giving you a local anaesthetic
Bu dişi doldurmam/ çekmem/törp lemem gerekiyor	I'll have to fill/pull this tooth/file this...down
Dişinizi delmem gerekiyor	I'll have to drill
Ağzünüzü açün	Open wide, please
Ağzünüzü kapayün	Close your mouth, please
Ağzünüzü çalkalayün	Rinse, please
Hala ağrüyor mu?	Does it hurt still?

My filling's come out ____	**Dolgum düştü**
	dolgoom dewshtew
I've got a broken crown __	**Dişimin köprüsü kırıldı**
	dishimin kurpRewsew kuhRuhlduh
I'd like/I don't want a ____ local anaesthetic	**Lokal anestezi istiyorum/istemiyorum**
	lokal anestezi istiyoRoom/istemiyoRoom
Can you do a makeshift__ repair job?	**Bana bir müddet idare edecek şekilde yardım edebilir misiniz?**
	bana biR mewd-det idaRe edejek shekildeh yaRduhm edebiliR misiniz?
I don't want this tooth ____ pulled	**Bu dişin çekilmesini istemiyorum**
	boo dishin chekilmesini istemiyoRoom
My dentures are broken. _ Can you fix them?	**Takma dişim kırıldı. Tamir edebilir misiniz?**
	*takma dishim kuhRuhlduh. **tah**mir edebiliR misiniz?*

14.1 Asking for help

Help! _____	**İmdat!**
	imdat!
Fire! _____	**Yangın!**
	yanguhn!
Police! _____	**Polis!**
	polis!
Quick! _____	**Çabuk!**
	chabook!
Danger! _____	**Tehlike!**
	teHlikeh!
Watch out! _____	**Dikkat!**
	dik-kat!
Stop! _____	**Dur!**
	dooR
Be careful! _____	**Dikkat et!**
	dik-kat et!
Don't!_____	**Yapma!**
	yapma!
Let go!_____	**Bırak!**
	buhRak!
Stop that thief!_____	**Hırsız var, yakalayın!**
	huhRsuhz vaR, yakala-yuhn!
Could you help me, _____ please?	**Bana yardım eder misiniz?**
	bana yaRduhm edeR misiniz?
Where's the police _____ station/emergency exit/fire escape?	**Karakol/acil çıkış/yangın merdiveni nerede?**
	kaRakol/ah-jil chuhkuhsh/yanguhn meRdiveni neredeh?
Where's the nearest fire __ extinguisher?	**Yangın söndürücüsü nerede?**
	yanguhn surndewRewjewsew neRedeh?
Call the fire brigade! _____	**İtfaiyeyi çağırın!**
	itfah-iyeyi cha:uhRuhn!
Call the police!_____	**Polisi arayın**
	polisi aRa-yuhn

Call an ambulance! _____	**Bir ambülans çağırın**
	biR ambewlans cha:uhRuhn
Where's the nearest _____ phone?	**Telefon nerede?**
	telefon neRedeh?
Could I use your phone? _	**Telefonunuzu kullanabilir miyim?**
	telefonoonoozoo kool-lanabiliR miyim?
What's the emergency ___ number?	**Acil servis numarası ne?**
	***ah-jil** seRvis noomaRasuh neh?*
What's the number for ___ the police?	**Karakolun telefon numarası ne?**
	kaRakoloon telefon noomaRasuh neh?

14.2 LOSS

I've lost my purse/ _____ wallet	**Cüzdanımı/evrak çantamı kaybettim**
	jewzdanuhm/evRak chantamuh kíbet-tim
I lost my...yesterday _____	**Dün...unuttum**
	dewn...oonoot-toom
I left my...here _____	**...buraya bırakmıştım**
	...booRa-ya buhRakmuhshtuhm
Did you find my...? _____	**Benim...buldunuz mu?**
	benim...booldoonooz moo?
It was right here _____	**Buradaydı**
	booRadíduh
It's quite valuable _____	**Çok değerli**
	chok de:eRli
Where's the lost_____ property office?	**Kayıp eşya bürosu nerede?**
	kí-uhp eshya bewRosoo neRedeh?

14.3 Accidents

There's been an accident	**Bir kaza oldu**
	biR kaza oldoo
Someone's fallen into _____ the water	**Biri suya düştü**
	biRi sooya dewshtew
There's a fire _____	**Yangın var**
	yanguhn vaR
Is anyone hurt? _____	**Yaralanan var mı?**
	yaRalanan vaR muh?
Some people have _____ been/no one's been injured	**Yaralı var (yok)**
	yaRaluh vaR (yok)
There's someone in _____ the car/train still	**Arabada/trende biri daha var**
	aRabada/trendeh biRi da-ha vaR
It's not too bad. Don't ___ worry	**Pek bir şey yok. Merak etmeyin**
	pek biR shey yok. meRak etmeyin
Leave everything the _____ way it is, please	**Hiç bir şeyin yerini değiştirmeyiniz**
	hich biR sheyin yeRini de:ishtiRmeyiniz
I want to talk to the _____ police first	**Önce polisle görüşmek istiyorum**
	urnjeh polisleh gurRewshmek istiyoRoom
I want to take a _____ photo first	**Önce bir fotoğraf çekmek istiyorum**
	urnjeh biR foto:Raf chekmek istiyoRoom
Here's my name _____ and address	**Buyurun, adım ve adresim**
	booy-ooRoon aduhm ve adResim
Could I have your _____ name and address?	**Adınızı ve adresinizi alabilir miyim?**
	aduhnuhzuh ve adResinizi alabiliR miyim?
Could I see some _____ dentification/your insurance papers?	**Nüfus cüzdanınızı/sigorta poliçenizi görebilir miyim?**
	newfoos cewzdanuhnuhz/sigoRta polichenizi gurRebiliR miyim?
Will you act as a _____ witness?	**Görgü tanıklığı eder misiniz?**
	gurRgew tanuhkluh:uh edeR misiniz?
I need the details for ____ the insurance	**Verileri sigorta için bilmem gerek**
	veRileRi sigoRta ichin bilmem geRek

Are you insured? _____	**Sigortalı mısınız?**
	sigoRtaluh muhsuhnuhz?
Third party or _____	**Tek taraflı mı yoksa çift taraflı mı?**
comprehensive?	*tek taRafluh muh yoksa chift taRafluh muh?*
Could you sign here, ____	**Burayı imzalar mısınız?**
please?	*booRaya imzalaR muhsuhnuhz?*

14.4 Theft

I've been robbed _____	**Soyuldum**
	soyooldoom
My...has been stolen ____	**...çalındı**
	...chaluhnduh
My car's been _____	**Arabama zorla girildi**
broken into	*aRabama zoRla giRildi*

14.5 Missing person

I've lost my child/ _____	**Çocuğumu/büyük annemi kaybettim**
grandmother	*chojoo:uhmuh/bew-yewk an-nemi kíbet-tim*
Could you help me _____	**Aramama yardım eder misiniz?**
find him/her?	*aRamama yaRduhm edebiliR misiniz?*
Have you seen a _____	**Küçük bir çocuk gördünüz mü?**
small child?	*kewchewk biR chojook gurRdewnewz*
	mew?
He's/she's...years old ____	**...yaşında**
	...yashuhnda
He's/she's got _____	**Kısa/uzun/sarı/kızıl/kahverengi/siyah/**
short/long/blond/red/	**beyaz/dalgalı/düz/kıvırcık saçlı**
brown/black/grey/curly/	*kuhsa/oozoon/saruh/kuhzuhl/kaHveRengi/*
straight/frizzy hair	*siyah/beyaz/dalgaluh/dewz/kuhvuhRjuhk*
	sachluh
with a ponytail _____	**saçı at kuyruklu**
	sachuh at kooyRookloo

with plaits	**saçı örgülü**
	sachuh urRgewlew
in a bun	**saçı topuz**
	sachuh topooz
He's/she's got blue/brown/green eyes	**Gözleri mavi/kahverengi/yeşil**
	gurzleRi mavi/kaHveRengi/yeshil
He's wearing swimming trunks/mountaineering boots	**Üzerinde mayosu/ayağında dağcılık ayakkabıları vardı**
	ewzeRindeh mayosoo/a-ya:uhnda da:juhluhk a-yak-kabuhlaRuh vaRduh
with/without glasses/ a bag	**gözlüklü/gözlüksüz/çantalı/çantasız**
	gurzlewklew/gurzlewksewz/chantaluh/ chantasuhz
tall/short	**kısa/uzun boylu**
	kuhsa/oozoon boyloo
This is a photo of him/her	**Bu onun resmi**
	boo onoon resmi
He/she must be lost	**Eminim kayboldu**
	eminim kíboldoo

14.6 The police

An arrest

I don't speak Turkish	**Türkçe konuşmasını bilmiyorum**
	tewRkcheh konooshmasuhnuh bilmiyoRoom
I didn't see the sign	**Levhayı görmedim**
	levha-yuh gurRmedim
I don't understand what it says	**Ne demek istendiğini anlamıyorum**
	neh demek istedi:ini anlamuhyoRoom
I was only doing... kilometres an hour	**Saatte...kilometre ile gidiyordum**
	saht-teh...kilometReh ileh gidiyoRdoom
I'll have my car checked	**Arabama baktıracağım**
	aRabama baktuhRaja:uhm

Ruhsatınız lütfen	Your registration papers, please
Arabanızı çok süratli kullanıyordunuz	You were speeding
Yanlış park etmişsiniz	You're not allowed to park here
Park ücretini ödememişsiniz	You haven't put money in the meter
Işıklarınız yanmıyo	Your lights aren't working
...liralık bir ceza ödemek zorundasınız	That's a...lira fine
Şimdi ödemek ister misiniz?	Do you want to pay on the spot?
Şimdi ödemek zorundasınız	You'll have to pay on the spot

I was blinded by _____ oncoming lights

Karşıdan gelen araç yüzünden bir şey göremez oldum
kaRshuhdan gelen aRach yewzewnden biR shey gurRemez oldoom

At the police station

I want to report a _____ collision/missing person/rape

Bir çarpışma/kayıp/tecavüz nedeniyle zabıt tutturmak istiyorum
biR chaRpuhshma/kí-uhp/tejahvewz nedeniyleh zabuht toot-tooRmak istiyoRoom

Could you make out_____ a report, please?

Tutanağa geçirir misiniz?
tootana:a gechiRiR misiniz?

Could I have a copy _____ for the insurance?

Bir nüshasını sigorta için alabilir miyim?
biR news-hasuhnuh sigoRta ichin alabiliR miyim?

I've lost everything _____

Her şeyimi kaybettim
heR sheyimi kíbet-tim

I've run out of money____

Param bitti, ne yapacağımı bilmiyorum
paRam bit-ti, neh yapaja:uhmuh bilmiyoRoom

Can you lend me some __ money	**Bir miktar borç para verebilir misiniz?**
	biR miktaR boRch paRa veRebiliR misiniz?
I'd like an interpreter ____	**Tercüman istiyorum**
	teRjewman istiyoRoom
I'm innocent _____	**Ben suçsuzum**
	ben soochsoozoom
I don't know anything____ about it	**Benim hiç bir şeyden haberim yok**
	benim hich biR sheyden habeRim yok
I want to speak to_____ someone from the British consulate	**İngiltere konsolosluğundan biri ile görüşmek istiyorum**
	ingiltere konsoslooːoondan biRi ileh gurRewshmek istiyoRoom
I need to see someone __ from the British embassy	**İngiltere büyük elçiliğinden biri ile görüşmek istiyorum**
	ingiltere bew-yewk elchiliːinden biRi ileh gurRewshmek istiyoRoom
I want a lawyer who ____ speaks English	**İngilizce konuşmasını bilen bir avukat istiyorum**
	ingilizjeh konooshmasuhnuh bilen biR avookat istiyoRoom

Nerede oldu?	Where did it happen?
Ne kaybettiniz?	What's missing?
Ne çalındı?	What's been taken?
Nüfus cüzdanınızı görebilir miyim?	Could I see some identification?
Saat kaçta oldu?	What time did it happen?
Başka kimlerin ilişkisi var?	Who was involved?
Görgü tanıkları var mı?	Are there any witnesses?
Bunu doldurur musunuz?	Fill this out, please
Burayı imzalayın lütfen	Sign here, please
Tercüman ister misiniz?	Do you want an interpreter?

Word list English – Turkish 158

Word list English – Turkish

● **This word list** is meant to supplement the previous chapters.
In a number of cases, words not contained in this list can be found
elsewhere in this book, namely in the lists of the parts of the car,
the bicycle and the tent. Many food terms can be found in the
Turkish–English list in 4.7.

A

about	yaklaşık olarak	yaklashuhk olaRak
above	...üstünde	...ewstewndeh
abroad	yurt dışı	yooRt duhshuh
accident	kaza	kaza
adder	engerek yılanı	engeRek yuhlanuh
addition	toplama	toplama
address	adres	adRes
admission	giriş	giRish
admission price	giriş fiyatı	giRish fiyatuh
advice	öneri, tavsiye	urneRi, tavsiyeh
after	sonra	sonRa
afternoon (in the)	öğleden sonra	ur:leden sonRa
aftershave	tıraş losyonu	tuhRash los-yonoo
again	yeniden	yeniden
against	karşı	kaRshuh
age	yaş	yash
Aids	Aids hastalığı	eehds hastaluh:uh
air conditioning	havalandırma	havalanduhRma
air mattress	şişirme yatak	shishiRmeh yatak
air sickness bag	istifrağ torbası	istifra: toRbasuh
aircraft	uçak	oochak
airmail, by	uçak ile	uchak ileh
airport	havaalanı	havaalanuh
alarm	alarm	alaRm
alarm clock	çalarsaat	chalaRsaht
alcohol	alkol	alkol

all the time	daima	*díma*
allergic	alerjik	*aleRzhik*
alone	yalnız	*yalnuhz*
always	her zaman	*heR zaman*
ambulance	ambülans	*ambewlans*
amount	miktar	*miktaR*
amusement park	lunapark	*loona-paRk*
anaesthetize	uyuşturmak	*ooyooshtooRmak*
anchovy	hamsi	*hamsi*
and	ve	*veh*
angry	kızgın	*kuhzguhn*
animal	hayvan	*hívan*
ankle	ayak bileği	*a-yak bile:i*
answer	cevap, yanıt	*jevap, yanuht*
ant	karınca	*kaRuhnja*
antibiotics	antibiyotik	*antibiyotik*
antifreeze	antifriz	*antifRiz*
antique	antika	*antika*
antiques	antika	*antika*
anus	anüs	*anews*
apartment	apartman dairesi	*apaRtman díResi*
aperitif	aperatif	*apeRatif*
apologize	özür dilemek	*urzewR dilemek*
apple	elma	*elma*
apple juice	elma suyu	*elma soo-yoo*
apple pudding	elma tatlısı	*elma tatluhsuh*
apple sauce	elma sosu	*elma sosoo*
appointment	randevu	*randevoo*
apricot	kayısı	*kí-uhsuh*
April	nisan	*nisan*
architecture	mimarlık	*mimaRluhk*
area	civar	*jivaR*
area code	şehirlerarası	*sheh-hiRleR-aRasuh*
	kod numarası	*kod noomaRasuh*
arm	kol	*kol*
arrange	sözleşmek	*surzleshmek*
arrive	varmak	*vaRmak*

arrow	ok	*ok*
art	sanat	*sanat*
artery	atardamar	*ataRdamaR*
artichokes	enginar	*enginaR*
article	malzeme	*malzemeh*
artificial respiration	suni tenefüs	*sooni tenefews*
ashtray	kül tablası	*kewl tablasuh*
ask	sormak	*soRmak*
ask	rica etmek	*rija etmek*
asparagus	kuşkonmaz	*kooshkonmaz*
aspirin	aspirin	*aspiRin*
assault	sarkıntılık	*saRkuhntuhluhk*
at night	geceleyin	*gejeleyin*
at the back	arkada	*aRkada*
at the front	önde	*urndeh*
aubergine	patlıcan	*patluhjan*
August	ağustos	*a:oostos*
automatic	otomatik	*otomatik*
autumn	sonbahar	*sonba-haR*
avalanche	çığ	*chuh*
awake	uyanık	*ooyanuhk*
awning	güneşlik	*gewneshlik*

B

baby	bebek	*bebek*
baby food	bebek maması	*bebek mamasuh*
babysitter	çocuk bakıcısı	*chojook bakuhjuhsuh*
back	sırt	*suhRt*
backpack	sırt çantası	*suhRt chantasuh*
bad	kötü	*kurtew*
bag	çanta	*chanta*
baker	fırın	*fuhRuhn*
balcony (theatre)	loca	*loja*
balcony (to building)	balkon	*balkon*
ball	top	*top*
ballet	bale	*baleh*

ballpoint pen	tükenmez kalem	*tewkenmez kalem*
banana	muz	*mooz*
bandage	sargı	*saRguh*
bank (river)	sahil	*sa-hil*
bank	banka	*banka*
bank card	banka kartı	*banka kaRtuh*
bar (café)	bar	*baR*
bar (drinks cabinet)	minibar	*minibaR*
barbecue	mangal	*mangal*
bath	banyo	*banyo*
bath attendant	cankurtaran	*jankooRtaRan*
bath foam	banyo köpüğü	*banyo kurpew:ew*
bath towel	banyo havlusu	*banyo havloosoo*
bathing cap	bone	*boneh*
bathing cubicle	banyo kabini	*banyo kabini*
bathing suit	mayo	*ma-yo*
bathroom	banyo	*banyo*
battery	pil	*pil*
battery (car)	akümülatör	*akewmewlaturR*
beach	plaj	*plazh*
beans	(kuru) fasulye	*(kooRoo) fasoolyeh*
beautiful	güzel	*gewzel*
beauty parlour	güzellik merkezi	*gewzel-lik meRkezi*
bed	yatak	*yatak*
bee	arı	*aRuh*
beef	sığır eti	*suh:uhR eti*
beer	bira	*biRa*
beetroot	pancar	*panjaR*
begin	başlamak	*bashlamak*
beginner	yeni başlayan	*yeni bashla-yan*
behind	...arkasında	*...aRkasuhnda*
belt	kemer	*kemeR*
berth	kuşet	*kooshet*
better	daha iyi	*da-ha iyi*
bicarbonate of soda	karbonat	*kaRbonat*
bicycle	bisiklet	*bisiklet*
bicycle pump	bisiklet pompası	*bisiklet pompasuh*

bicycle repairman	bisiklet tamircisi	*bisiklet tahmiRjisi*
bikini	bikini	*bikini*
bill	hesap	*hesap*
billiards, to play	bilardo oynamak	*bilaRdo oynamak*
birthday	doğum günü	*do:oom gewnew*
biscuit	bisküvi	*biskwi*
bite	ısırmak	*uhsuhRmak*
bitter	acı	*ajuh*
black	siyah	*si-yaH*
bland	tatsız	*tatsuhz*
blanket	battaniye	*bat-taniyeh*
bleach	ağartmak	*a:aRtmak*
blister	su toplaması	*soo toplamasuh*
blond	sarışın	*saRuhshuhn*
blood	kan	*kan*
blood pressure	tansiyon	*tansiyon*
blouse	bluz	*blooz*
blow dry	saç kurutma	*sach kooRootma*
blue	mavi	*mavi*
blunt	kör	*kurR*
boat	gemi, vapur	*gemi, vapooR*
body	vücut	*vewjoot*
body milk	vücut losyonu	*vewjoot losyonoo*
boiled	haşlanmış	*hashlanmuhs*
boiled ham	jambon	*zhambon*
bonbon	şekerleme	*shekeRlemeh*
bone	kemik	*kemik*
bonnet	motor kapağı	*motoR kapa:uh*
book (verb)	yer ayırtmak	*yeR a-yuhRtmak*
book	kitap	*kitap*
book	yer ayırtmak	*yeR a-yuhRtmak*
booked	rezerveli	*rezeRveli*
booking office	bilet gişesi	*bilet gishesi*
bookshop	kitabevi	*kitabevi*
border	sınır	*suhnuhR*
bored, to be	sıkılmak	*suhkuhlmak*
boring	can sıkıcı	*jan suhkuhjuh*

born	doğumlu	do:oomloo
borrow	borç almak	boRch almak
botanical gardens	botanik bahçesi	botanik baHchesi
both	her ikisi	heR ikisi
bottlewarmer	biberon ısıtıcı	bibeRon uhsuhtuhjuh
bottle (baby's)	biberon	bibeRon
box	kutu	kootoo
box	loca	loja
boy	oğlan	o:lan
bra	sutyen	soot-yen
bracelet	bilezik	bilezik
brake	fren	fFen
brake fluid	fren sıvısı	fFen suhvuhsuh
brake oil	fren yağı	fFen ya:uh
brass	pirinç	piRinch
bread	ekmek	ekmek
break	kırmak	kuhRmak
breakfast	kahvaltı	kaHvaltuh
breast	göğüs	gur:ews
bridge	köprü	kurpRew
briefs	külot	kewlot
bring	getirmek	getiRmek
brochure	broşür	bRoshewR
broken	bozuk	bozook
brother	erkek kardeş	eRkek kaRdesh
brown	kahverengi	kaHveh-Rengi
bruise	berelemek	beRelemek
brush	fırça	fuhRcha
Brussels sprouts	Brüksel lahanası	bRewksel la-hanasuh
bucket	kova	kova
bug	mikrop	mikRop
bugs	böcek	burjek
building	bina	bina
buoy	şamandıra	shamanduhRa
burglary	hırsızlık	huhRsuhzluhk
burn	yanmak	yanmak
burnt	yanık	yanuhk

bus	otobüs	*otobews*
bus station	otogar	*otogaR*
bus stop	otobüs durağı	*otobews dooRa:uh*
business class	birinci sınıf	*biRinji suhnuhf*
business trip	iş seyahati	*ish seya-hati*
busy	kalabalık	*kalabuhluk*
butane camping gas	bütan kamp gazı	*bewtan kamp gazuh*
butcher	kasap	*kasap*
butter	tereyağı	*teRe-ya:uh*
buttered roll	tereyağılı ufak ekmek	*teRe-ya:uhluh oofak ekmek*
button	düğme	*dew:meh*
buy	satın almak	*satuhn almak*

C

cabbage	lahana	*la-hana*
cabin	kamara	*kamaRa*
cake	pasta	*pasta*
cake shop	pastane	*pastaneh*
call	telefon etmek	*telefon etmek*
called, to be	adlı	*adluh*
camera	fotoğraf makinesi	*foto:Raf makinesi*
camp	kamp kurmak	*kamp kooRmak*
camp shop	kamp malzemeleri satan mağaza	*kamp malzemeleRi satan ma:aza*
camp site	kamping, kamp sahası	*kamping, kamp sa-hasuh*
camper	kamper	*kampeR*
campfire	kamp ateşi	*kamp ateshi*
camping guide	kamp kılavuzu	*kamp kuhla-oozoo*
camping permit	kamp kurma ruhsatı	*kamp kooRma rooHsatuh*
canal boat	gezi vapuru	*gezi vapooRoo*
cancel	iptal etmek	*iptahl etmek*
candle	mum	*moom*
canoe (verb)	kano yapmak	*kano yapmak*

canoe	kano	*kano*
car	araba, otomobil	*aRaba, otomobil*
carriage	vagon	*vagon*
car deck	otomobil guvertesi	*otomobil gewveRtesi*
car documents	araba ruhsat belgeleri	*aRaba rooHsat belgeleRi*
car seat	araba koltuğu	*aRaba koltoo:oo*
car trouble	motor arızası	*motoR aRuhzasuh*
carafe	sürahi	*sewRah-hi*
caravan	karavan	*kaRavan*
cardigan	hırka	*huhRka*
careful	dikkatli	*dik-katli*
carrot	havuç	*havooch*
carton	karton	*kaRton*
cascade	şelale	*shelaleh*
cash desk	kasa	*kasa*
casino	kumarhane	*koomaRhaneh*
cassette	kaset	*kaset*
castle	kale	*kaleh*
cat	kedi	*kedi*
catalogue	katalog	*katalog*
cauliflower	karnıbahar	*kaRnuhba-haR*
cave	mağara	*ma:aRa*
CD	kompakt disk	*kompakt disk*
celebrate	kutlamak	*kootlamak*
cellotape	selobant	*selobant*
cemetery	mezarlık	*mezahRluhk*
centimetre	santimetre	*santimetReh*
central heating	kalorifer	*kaloRifeR*
centre	orta	*oRta*
centre	merkez	*meRkez*
chair	sandalye	*sandal-yeh*
chambermaid	oda hizmetçisi	*oda hizmetchisi*
champagne	şampanya	*shampan-ya*
change (coins)	bozuk para	*bozook paRa*
change (verb)	değiştirmek	*de:ishtiRmek*
change (trains, buses)	aktarmak	*aktaRmak*

change (money)	para bozdurmak	*paRa bozdooRmak*
change the baby's nappy	bebe:in altını değiştirmek	*bebe:in altuhnuh de:ishtiRmek*
change the oil	yağ değiştirmek	*ya: de:ishtiRmek*
charter flight	çarter uçuş	*chaRteR oochoosh*
chat up	flört etmek	*flurRt etmek*
check	kontrol etmek	*kontRol etmek*
check in	yolcu kabul	*yoljoo kabool*
cheers	şerefe	*sheRefeh*
cheese (tasty, mild)	peynir (lezzetli, hafif)	*peyniR (lez-zetli, hafif)*
chef	şef	*shef*
chemist	eczane	*ejzaneh*
cheque	çek	*chek*
cherries	kiraz	*kiRaz*
chess, to play	satranç oynamak	*satRanch oynamak*
chewing gum	sakız, çiklet	*sakuhz, chiklet*
chicken	tavuk	*tavook*
child	çocuk	*chojook*
child's seat	çocuk oturacağı	*chojook otooRaja:uh*
chilled	soğutulmuş	*so:ootoolmoosh*
chin	çene	*cheneh*
chips	patates kızartması	*patates kuhzaRtmasuh*
chocolate	çikolata	*chikolata*
choose	seçmek	*sechmek*
chop	pirzola	*piRzola*
cigar	puro	*pooRo*
cigar shop	tütüncü	*tewtewnjew*
cigarette	sigara	*sigaRa*
cigarette paper	sigara kağıdı	*sigaRa ka:uhduh*
cine camera	film makinesi	*film makinesi*
circle	daire, çember	*díReh, chembeR*
circus	sirk	*siRk*
city	şehir	*she-hiR*
city map	şehir haritası	*she-hiR haRitasuh*
classical concert	klasik konser	*klasik konseR*
clean (verb)	temizlemek	*temizlemek*

clean	temiz	_temiz_
clear	net	_net_
clearance	indirimli satışlar	_indiRimli satuhshlaR_
clock	duvar saati	_doovaR sahti_
closed	kapalı	_kapaluh_
closed off	kapalı (yol)	_kapaluh (yol)_
clothes	konfeksiyon	_konfeksiyon_
clothes hanger	askı	_askuh_
clothes peg	mandal	_mandal_
clothing	giyim	_giyim_
coat	palto	_palto_
cockroach	hamam böceği	_hamam burje:i_
cocoa	kakao	_kaka-o_
cod	morina balığı	_moRina baluh:uh_
coffee	kahve	_kaHveh_
coffee filter	kahve filtresi	_kaHveh filtResi_
cognac	konyak	_kon-yak_
cold	soğuk	_so:ook_
cold (medical)	soğuk algınlığı	_so:ook alguhnluh:uh_
cold cuts	salam çeşitleri	_salam cheshitleRi_
collarbone	köprücük kemiği	_kurpRewjewk kemi:i_
colleague	meslektaş	_meslektash_
collision	çarpışma	_chaRpuhshma_
cologne	kolonya	_kolon-ya_
colour	renk	_renk_
colour pencils	boya kalemi	_boya kalemi_
colour TV	renkli televizyon	_renkli televizyon_
colouring book	boyama kitabı	_boyama kitabuh_
comb	tarak	_taRak_
come	gelmek	_gelmek_
come back	geri gelmek	_geRi gelmek_
compartment	kompartman	_kompaRtman_
complain (verb)	şikayetçi olmak	_shika-yet-chi olmak_
complaint	şikayet	_shika-yet_
complaints book	şikayet defteri	_shika-yet defteRi_
completely	tamamen	_tamahmen_
compliment	iltifat	_iltifat_

compulsory	mecburi, zorunlu	*mejbooRi, zoRoonloo*
concert	konser	*konseR*
concert hall	konser salonu	*konseR salonoo*
concussion	beyin sarsıntısı	*beyin saRsuhntuhsuh*
condom	prezervatif	*pReseRvatif*
congratulate	tebrik etmek	*tebRik etmek*
connection	bağlantı	*ba:lantuh*
constipation	kabızlık	*kabuhzluhk*
consulate	konsolosluk	*konsoloslook*
consultation	konsültasyon	*konsewltas-yon*
contact lens	kontak lens	*kontak lens*
contact lens solution	lens bakım	*lens bakuhm*
	solüsyonu	*solews-yonoo*
contagious	bulaşıcı	*boolashuhjuh*
contraceptive	doğum kontrol	*do:oom*
	metodu	*kontRol metodoo*
contraceptive pill	doğum kontrol	*do:oom kontRol hapuh*
	hapı	
cook (verb)	pişirmek	*pishiRmek*
cook	aşçı	*ash-chuh*
copper	bakır	*bakuhR*
copy	kopya nüsha	*kop-ya news-ha*
corkscrew	tirbuşon	*tiRbooshon*
corner	köşe	*kursheh*
cornflour	mısır unu	*muhsuhR oonoo*
correct	doğru	*do:Roo*
correspond	yazışmak	*yazuhshmak*
corridor	koridor	*koRidoR*
costume	kostüm	*kostewm*
cot	çocuk karyolası	*chojook kaR-yolasuh*
cotton	pamuklu	*pamookloo*
cotton wool	idrofil pamuk	*idRofil pamook*
cough	öksürük	*urksewRewk*
cough mixture	öksürük şurubu	*urksewRewk*
		shooRooboo
counter	tezgah	*tezgahH*
country	ülke	*ewlkeh*

country (countryside)	taşra	*tashRa*
country code	ülke telefon kodu	*ewlkeh telefon kodoo*
courgette	kabak	*kabak*
course	tedavi	*tedavi*
cousin	kuzen	*koozen*
crab	yengeç	*yengech*
cream	kaymak	*kímak*
credit card	kredi kartı	*kRedi kaRtuh*
crisps	patates çipsi	*patates chipsi*
croissant	kruason (Fransız kahvaltı böreği)	*kRooason (fRansuhz kaHvaltuh burRe:i)*
crosscountry run	kır koşusu	*kuhR koshoosoo*
cross the road	karşıya geçmek	*kaRshuhya gechmek*
crossing	yaya geçidi	*yaya gechidi*
crossing	geçiş	*gechish*
cry	ağlamak	*a:lamak*
cubic metre	metre küp	*metReh kewp*
cucumber	salatalık	*salataluhk*
cuddly toy	oyuncak hayvan	*oyoonjak hayvan*
cuff links	manşet düğmeleri	*manshet dew:meleRi*
culottes	pantolon etek	*pantalon etek*
cup	fincan	*finjan*
curly	kıvırcık	*kuhvuhRjuhk*
current	akıntı	*akuhntuh*
cushion	yastık	*yastuhk*
custard	krema	*kRema*
customary	normal	*noRmal*
customs	gümrük	*gewmRewk*
customs check	gümrük kontrolü	*gewmRewk kontRolew*
cut	kesmek	*kesmek*
cut	kesmek	*kesmek*
cutlery	çatal bıçak takımı	*chatal buhchak takuhmuh*
cycling	bisiklet sporu	*bisiklet spoRoo*

dairy	süt mamülleri dükkanı	*sewt mamewl-leRi dewk-kahnuh*
damaged	hasara uğramış	*hasaRa oo:Ramuhsh*
dance	dans etmek	*dans etmek*
dandruff	kepek	*kepek*
danger	tehlike	*teHlikeh*
dangerous	tehlikeli	*teHlikeli*
dark	karanlık	*kaRanluhk*
date	randevu	*randevoo*
daughter	kız	*kuhz*
day	gün	*gewn*
day after tomorrow	yarın değil öbür gün	*yaRuhn de:il urbewR gewn*
day before yesterday	evvelki gün	*ev-velki gewn*
dead	ölü	*urlew*
decaffeinated	kafeinsiz	*kafeynsiz*
December	aralık	*aRaluhk*
deck chair	şezlong	*shezlong*
declare (customs)	beyan etmek	*beyahn etmek*
deep	derin	*deRin*
deep sea diving	deniz dalgıçlığı	*deniz dalguhchluh:uh*
deepfreeze	dondurucu	*dondooRoojoo*
degrees	derece	*deRejeh*
delay	rötar	*rurtaR*
delicious	nefis	*nefis*
dentist	dişçi	*dishchi*
dentures	takma diş	*takma dish*
deodorant	deodorant	*deodorant*
department	reyon	*reyon*
department store	büyük mağaza	*bewyewk ma:aza*
departure	gidiş	*gidish*
departure time	gidiş saati	*gidish sahti*
depilatory cream	tüy dökücü krem	*tewy durkewjew kRem*
deposit (verb)	emanete vermek	***emahneteh** veRmek*
deposit	kaparo	*kapaRo*

dervish dancers	semazenler	*semazenleR*
dessert	tatlı	*tatluh*
destination	gidilen yer	*gidilen yeR*
develop	banyo etmek	*banyo etmek*
diabetic	şeker hastası	*shekeR hastasuh*
dial	çevirmek	*cheviRmek*
diamond	elmas	*elmas*
diarrhoea	ishal	*is-hal*
dictionary	sözlük	*surzlewk*
diesel	dizel	*dizel*
diesel oil	mazot	*mazot*
diet	perhiz	*peRhiz*
difficulty	zorluk	*zoRlook*
dining room	yemek salonu	*yemek salonoo*
dining/buffet car	yemekli vagon	*yemekli vagon*
dinner	akşam yemeği	*aksham yeme:i*
dinner jacket	smokin	*smokin*
dinner, to have	akşam yemeği	*aksham yeme:i*
	yemek	*yemek*
direction	yön	*yurn*
directly	dosdoğru	*dosdo:Roo*
dirty	kirli	*kiRli*
disabled	sakat	*sakat*
disco	diskotek	*diskotek*
discount	indirim	*indiRim*
dish	yemek	*yemek*
dish of the day	günün yemeği	*gewnewn yeme:i*
disinfectant	dezenfekte edici	*dezenfekteh ediji*
distance	mesafe	*mesafeh*
distilled water	arı su	*aruh soo*
disturb	rahatsız etmek	*ra-hatsuhz etmek*
disturbance	rahatsızlık	*ra-hatsuhzluhk*
dive	dalmak	*dalmak*
diving	dalgıçlık sporu	*dalguhchluhk spoRoo*
diving board	tramplen	*tRamplen*
diving gear	dalgıçlık takımı	*dalguhchluhk takuhmuh*
divorced	boşanmış	*boshanmuhsh*

dizziness	baş dönmesi	bash durnmesi
do	yapmak	yapmak
doctor	doktor	doktoR
dog	köpek	kurpek
doll	oyuncak bebek	oynoojak bebek
domestic	yurt içi	yooRt ichi
done (well cooked)	pişmiş	pishmish
door	kapı	kapuh
double	iki kişilik	iki kishilik
down	aşağı	asha:uh
draught	cereyan	jeReyan
draughts, to play	dama oynamak	dama oynamak
dream	rüya görmek	rewya gurRmek
dress	elbise	elbiseh
dressing gown	sabahlık	sabaHluhk
drink	içecek	ichejek
drinking chocolate	kakaolu süt	kaka-oloo sewt
drinking water	içme suyu	ichmeh soo-yoo
drive	araba kullanmak	aRaba kool-lanmak
driver	şoför	shofurR
driving licence	ehliyet	eHliyet
drought	kuraklık	kooRakluhk
dry (verb)	kurutmak	kooRootmak
dry	kuru	kooRoo
dry clean	kuru temizleme	kooRoo temizlemeh
dry cleaner's	kuru temizleyici	kooRoo temizleyiji
dry shampoo	kuru saçlar için şampuan	kooRoo sachlaR ichin shampoo-an
dummy	yalancı meme	yalanjuh memeh
during	boyunca	boyoonja
during	esnasında	esnasuhnda
during the day	gündüz	gewndewz

ear	kulak	*koolak*
ear, nose and throat (ENT) specialist	kulak burun boğaz (KBB) uzmanı	*koolak booRoon bo:az oozmanuh*
earache	kulak ağrısı	*koolak a:Ruhsuh*
eardrops	kulak damlası	*koolak damlasuh*
early	erken	*eRken*
earrings	küpe	*kewpeh*
earth	toprak	*topRak*
earthenware	çömlek	*churmlek*
east	doğu	*do:oo*
easy	kolay	*kolí*
eat	yemek	*yemek*
eczema	egzama	*egzama*
eel	yılan balığı	*yuhlan baluh:uhn*
egg	yumurta	*yoomooRta*
elastic band	lastik bant	*lastik bant*
electric	elektrikli	*elektRikli*
electricity	elektrik	*elektRik*
embassy	büyük elçilik	*bewyewk elchilik*
emergency brake	acil fren	***ah-jil** fRen*
emergency exit	acil çıkış	***ah-jil** chuhkuhsh*
emergency number	acil servis numarası	***ah-jil** seRvis noomaRasuh*
emergency triangle	reflektör	*reflekturR*
emery board	tırnak törpüsü	*turRnak turRpewsew*
empty	boş	*bosh*
engaged	dolu	*doloo*
engaged	meşgul	*meshgool*
English language	İngilizce	*ingilizjeh*
enjoy	zevk almak	*zevk almak*
entertainment guide	etkinlik dergisi	*etkinlik deRgisi*
envelope	zarf	*zaRf*
evening	akşam	*aksham*
evening wear	gece kıyafeti	*gejeh kuhyafeti*
event	olay	*olí*

everything	her şey	her shey
everywhere	her yerde	heR yeRdeh
examine	muayene etmek	moo-a-yeneh etmek
excavation	arkeolojik kazı	aRkeolozhik kazuh
excellent	çok iyi	chok iyi
exchange	değiştirmek	de:ishtiRmek
exchange office	kambiyo bürosu	kambio bewRosoo
exchange rate	döviz kuru	durviz kooRoo
excursion	turistik gezi	tooRistik gezi
exhibition	sergi	seRgi
exit	çıkış	chuhkuhsh
expenses	masraf	masRaf
expensive	pahalı	pa-haluh
explain	açıklamak	achuhklamak
express train	mavi tren, ekspres	mavi tRen, ekspRes
external	dış	duhsh
eye	göz	gurz
eye drops	göz damlası	gurz damlasuh
eye shadow	göz boyası	gurz boyasuh
eye specialist	göz doktoru	gurz doktoRoo
eyeliner	göz kalemi	gurz kalemi

F

face	yüz	yewz
factory	fabrika	fabRika
fall	düşmek	dewshmek
family	aile	íleh
famous	ünlü, meşhur	ewnlew, mesh-hooR
far away	uzak	oozak
farewell	veda	veda
farm	çiftlik	chiftlik
farmer	çiftçi	chiftchi
farmer's wife	çiftçi kadın	chiftchi kaduhn
fashion	moda	moda
fast	çabuk	chabook
father	baba	baba

fault	hata	*hata*
fax, to send a	faks çekmek	*faks chekmek*
February	şubat	*shoobat*
feel	hissetmek	*his-setmek*
feel like	canı istemek	*januh istemek*
fence	çit	*chit*
ferry	vapur, feribot	*vapuR, feRibot*
fever	ateş	*atesh*
fill	dolgu yapmak	*dolgoo yapmak*
fill out	doldurmak	*doldooRmak*
filling (dental)	dolgu	*dolgoo*
film	film	*film*
filter	filtre	*filtReh*
find	bulmak	*boolmak*
fine	para cezası	*paRa jezasuh*
finger	parmak	*paRmak*
fire	ateş, yangın	*atesh, yanguhn*
fire brigade	itfaiye	*it**fa**-iyeh*
fire escape	yangın merdiveni	*yanguhn meRdiveni*
fire extinguisher	yangın söndürücüsü	*yanguhn surndewRewjewsew*
first	birinci	*biRinji*
first aid	ilk yardım	*ilk yaRduhm*
first class	birinci sınıf	*biRinji suhnuhf*
first name	ad	*ad*
fish (verb)	balık tutmak	*baluhk tootmak*
fish	balık	*baluhk*
fishing rod	olta	*olta*
fit	uymak	*ooymak*
fitness centre	spor merkezi	*spoR meRkezi*
fitness training	egzersiz	*egzeRsiz*
fitting room	kabin	*kabin*
fix	tamir etmek	*tahmiR etmek*
flag	bayrak	*bíRak*
flash bulb	flaş lambası	*flash lambasuh*
flash cube	flaş lambası	*flash lambasuh*
flash gun	flaş	*flash*

flat	apartman dairesi	*apaRtman diRResi*
flea market	bit pazarı	*bit pazaRuh*
flight	uçuş	*oochoosh*
flight number	uçuş numarası	*oochoosh noomaRasuh*
flood	sel	*sel*
floor	kat	*kat*
flour	un	*oon*
flu	grip	*gRip*
flyover	bağlantı yolu	*ba:lantuh yoloo*
fly (insect)	sinek	*sinek*
fly (verb)	uçmak	*oochmak*
fog	sis	*sis*
foggy, to be	sis basmak	*sis basmak*
folkloristic	folklorik	*folkloRik*
follow	takip etmek	*takip etmek*
food	gıda	*guhda*
food poisoning	gıda zehirlenmesi	*guhda zeh-hiRlenmesi*
foot	ayak	*a-yak*
for	için	*ichin*
for hire	kiralık	*kiRaluhk*
forbidden	yasak	*yasak*
forehead	alın	*aluhn*
foreign	yabancı	*yabanjuh*
forget	unutmak	*oonootmak*
fork	çatal	*chatal*
form	form	*foRm*
fort	hisar	*hisaR*
forward	yollamak	*yol-lamak*
fountain	çeşme	*cheshmeh*
frame	çerçeve	*cheRcheveh*
free (seat)	boş	*bosh*
free	bedava, ücretsiz	*bedahva, ewjRetsiz*
free time	boş zaman	*bosh zaman*
freeze	donmak	*donmak*
French bread	francala	*fRanjala*
French language	Fransızca	*fRansuhzja*
fresh	taze	*tazeh*

Friday	cuma	*jooma*
fried	kızartılmış	*kuhzaRtuhlmuhsh*
fried egg	yağda yumurta	*ya:da yoomooRta*
friend	arkadaş	*aRkadash*
friendly	candan, cana yakın	*jandan, jana yakuhn*
frightened	korkmuş	*koRkmoosh*
fringe	kakül	*kakewl*
front (at the)	ön tarafta	*urn taRafta*
fruit	meyva	*meyva*
fruit juice	meyva suyu	*meyva soo-yoo*
frying pan	tava	*tava*
full	dolu	*doloo*
fun	eğlence	*e:lenjeh*
funfair	lunapark	*loona-paRk*

G

gallery	galeri	*galeRi*
game	oyun	*oyoon*
garage	garaj	*gaRazh*
garbage bag	çöp torbası	*churp toRbasuh*
garden	bahçe	*baHcheh*
gastroenteritis	mide iltihabı	*mideh iltihahbuh*
gauze	gazlı bez	*gazluh bez*
gear	vites	*vites*
gel	jöle	*zhurleh*
German language	Almanca	*almanja*
get off	inmek	*inmek*
gift	hediye	*hediyeh*
gilt	yaldızlı	*yalduhzluh*
ginger	zencefil	*zenjefil*
girl	kız	*kuhz*
girlfriend	kız arkadaş	*kuhz aRkadash*
giro cheque	posta çeki	*posta cheki*
giro pass	posta çeki kartı	*posta cheki kaRtuh*
glacier	buzul	*boozool*
glass (tumbler)	bardak	*baRdak*

glasses (sun -)	gözlük	*gurzlewk*
	(güneş gözlüğü)	*(gewnesh gurzlew:ew)*
glide	planörle uçmak	*planurRleh oochmak*
glove	eldiven	*eldiven*
glue	tutkal	*tootkal*
gnat	sivrisinek	*sivRisinek*
go	gitmek	*gitmek*
go back	geri dönmek	*geRi durnmek*
go out	çıkmak	*chuhkmak*
goat's cheese	keçi peyniri	*kechi peyniRi*
gold	altın	*altuhn*
golf course	golf sahası	*golf sa-hasuh*
gone	kayıp	*ka-yuhp*
good afternoon	iyi günler	*iyi gewnleR*
good evening	iyi akşamlar	*yi akshamlaR*
good morning	günaydın	*gewníduhn*
good night	iyi geceler	*iyi gejeleR*
goodbye	hoşça kal	*hosh-cha kal*
gram	gram	*gRam*
grandchild	torun	*toRoon*
grandfather	dede	*dedeh*
grandmother	büyük anne	*bewyewk an-neh*
grape juice	üzüm suyu	*ewzewm soo-yoo*
grapefruit	greyfrut	*gReyfRoot*
grapes	üzüm	*ewzewm*
grave	mezar	*mezaR*
greasy	yağlı	*ya:luh*
green	yeşil	*yeshil*
green card	yeşil kart	*yeshil kaRt*
greet	selam vermek	*selahm veRmek*
grill	ızgara yapmak	*uhzgaRa yapmak*
grilled	kızartılmış	*kuhzaRtuhlmuhsh*
grocer	bakkal	*bak-kal*
ground	yer	*yeR*
group	gurup	*gooRoop*
guest house	pansiyon	*pansiyon*
guide (book)	kılavuz, rehber	*kuhla-ooz, reHbeR*

H

guide (person)	rehber	*reHbeR*
guided tour	rehberli tur	*reHbeRli tooR*
gynaecologist	kadın doktoru	*kaduhn doktoRoo*

hair	saç	*sach*
hairbrush	saç fırçası	*sach fuhRchasuh*
hairdresser	kuaför; berber	*koo-afurR, beRbeR*
hairpins	saç tokası	*sach tokasuh*
hairspray	saç spreyi	*sach spReyi*
half	yarım	*yaRuhm*
half	yarı	*yaRuh*
half full	yarı dolu	*yaruh doloo*
hammer	çekiç	*chekich*
hand	el	*el*
hand brake	el freni	*el fReni*
handbag	el çantası	*el chantasuh*
handkerchief	mendil	*mendil*
handmade	el işi	*el ishi*
happy	memnun	*memnoon*
harbour	liman	*liman*
hard	sert	*seRt*
hat	şapka	*shapka*
hay fever	saman nezlesi	*saman nezlesi*
hazelnut	fındık	*fuhnduhk*
head	baş	*bash*
headache	baş ağrısı	*bash a:Ruhsuh*
health	sağlık	*sa:luhk*
health food shop	doğal gıda satan dükkan	*do:al guhda satan dewk-kahn*
hear	duymak	*dooymak*
hearing aid	işitme cihazı	*ishitmeh ji-hazuh*
heart	kalp	*kalp*
heart patient	kalp hastası	*kalp hastasuh*
heat	sıcaklık	*suhjakluhk*
heater	kalorifer	*kaloRifeR*

179

heavy	ağır	*a:uhR*
heel	ayak topuğu	*a-yak topoo:oo*
heel	topuk	*topook*
hello	merhaba	*meRhaba*
helmet	kask	*kask*
help (verb)	yardım etmek	*yarduhm etmek*
help	yardım	*yaRduhm*
helping	porsiyon	*poRsiyon*
herbal tea	baharlı çay	*ba-haRluh chí*
herbs	baharat	*ba-haRat*
here	burada	*booRada*
here you are	buyurun	*booyooRoon*
herring	ringa balığı	*ringa baluh:uh*
high	yüksek	*yewksek*
high tide	kabarma	*kabaRma*
highchair	çocuk sandalyesi	*chojook sandaliyesi*
hiking	hiking	*híking*
hiking trip	gezi	*gezi*
hip	kalça	*kalcha*
hire	kiralamak	*kiRalamak*
hitchhike	otostop yapmak	*otostop yapmak*
hobby	hobi	*hobi*
holdup	soyulma	*soyoolma*
holiday (national)	bayram tatili	*bíRam tatili*
holiday	tatil	*tatil*
holiday house	yazlık	*yazluhk*
holiday park	tatil köyü	*tatil kuryew*
home, at	evde	*evdeh*
homesickness	özlem	*urzlem*
honest	dürüst	*dewRewst*
honey	bal	*bal*
horizontal	yatay	*yatí*
horrible	iğrenç	*i:Rench*
horse	at	*at*
hospital	hastane	*hastaneh*
hospitality	misafirperverlik	*misahfiR-peRveRlik*
hot	sıcak	*suhjak*

hotwater bottle	sıcak su torbası	*suhjak soo toRbasuh*
hot	acı	*ajuh*
hotel	otel	*otel*
hour	saat	*saht*
house	ev	*ev*
household items	ev eşyaları	*ev eshyalaRuh*
houses of parliament	parlamento binası	*paRlamento binahsuh*
housewife	ev kadını	*ev kaduhnuh*
how far?	ne kadar?	*neh kadaR?*
how long?	ne kadar uzak?	*neh kadaR oozak?*
how much?	ne kadar?	*neh kadaR?*
how?	nasıl?	*nasuhl?*
hundred grams	yüz gram	*yewz gRam*
hungry, to be	acıkmak	*ajuhkmak*
hurricane	kasırga	*kasuhRga*
hurry	acele	*ajeleh*
husband	eş	*esh*
hut	kulübe	*koolewbeh*
hyperventilation	hiper ventilasyon	*hipeR ventilas-yon*

I

ice cream	dondurma	*dondooRma*
ice cubes	buz parçası	*booz paRchasuh*
ice skate	buz pateni	*booz pateni*
idea	fikir	*fikiR*
identification	kimlik kartı, nüfus cüzdanı	*kimlik kaRtuh, newfoos cewzdanuh*
identify	kimliğini tespit etmek	*kimli:ini tespit etmek*
ignition key	kontak anahtarı	*kontak anaHtaRuh*
ill	hasta	*hasta*
illness	hastalık	*hastaluhk*
imagine	sanmak	*sanmak*
immediately	hemen	*hemen*
import duty	gümrük vergisi	*gewmRewk veRgisi*
impossible	imkansız	*imkahnsuhz*

in	Ñiçine; içinde	*...ichineh, ichindeh*
in the evening	akşamleyin	*akshamleyin*
included	dahil	**da**-*hil*
indicate	göstermek	*gursteRmek*
indicator	yön gösterici	*yurn gursteRiji*
inexpensive	ucuz	*oojooz*
infection (viral, bacterial)	enfeksiyon	*enfeksiyon*
inflammation	iltihap	*iltihap*
information	bilgi	*bilgi*
information office	danışma bürosu	*danuhshma bewRosoo*
injection	aşı, iğne	*ashuh, i:neh*
injured	yaralı	*yaRaluh*
inner ear	iç kulak	*ich koolak*
inner tube	iç lastik	*ich lastik*
innocent	suçsuz	*soochsooz*
insect	böcek	*burjek*
insect bite	böcek ısırması	*burjek uhsuhRmasuh*
insect repellant	sinek koruyucu	*sinek koRooyoojoo*
	krem	*kRem*
inside	...içinde	*...ichindeh*
insole	ayakkabının iç	*a-yak-kabuhnuhn ich*
	tabanı	*tabanuh*
instructions	kullanılış şekli	*kool-lanuhluhsh shekli*
insurance	sigorta	*sigoRta*
intermission	ara	*aRa*
international	uluslararası	*oolooslaRaRasuh*
interpreter	tercüman	*teRjooman*
intersection	kavşak	*kavshak*
introduce oneself	kendini tanıtmak	*kendini tanuhtmak*
invite	davet etmek	*davet etmek*
iodine	tentürdiyot	*tentewRdiyot*
iron (metal)	demir	*demiR*
iron (verb)	ütülemek	*ewtewlemek*
iron	ütü	*ewtew*
ironing board	ütü masası	*ewtew masasuh*
island	ada	*ada*

| Italian language | İtalyanca | *ital-yanja* |
| itch | kaşıntı | *kashuhntuh* |

J

jack	kriko	*kRiko*
jacket	ceket	*jeket*
jam	reçel	*rechel*
January	ocak	*ojak*
jaw	çene	*cheneh*
jellyfish	deniz anası	*deniz anasuh*
jeweller	kuyumcu	*kooyoomjoo*
jewellery	mücevherat	*mewjev-heRat*
jog	koşu yapmak	*koshoo yapmak*
joke	şaka	*shaka*
July	temmuz	*tem-mooz*
jump leads	marş kablosu	*maRsh kablosoo*
jumper	kazak	*kazak*
June	haziran	*haziRan*

K

key	anahtar	*anaHtaR*
kilo	kilo	*kilo*
kilometre	kilometre	*kilometReh*
king	kral	*kRal*
kiss (verb)	öpmek	*urpmek*
kiss	öpücük	*urpewjewk*
kitchen	mutfak	*mootfak*
knee	diz	*diz*
knee socks	diz altı çorap	*diz altuh choRap*
knife	bıçak	*buhchak*
knit	örgü örmek	*urRgew urRmek*
know	bilmek	*bilmek*

L

lace	dantel	*dantel*
lace	ayakkabı bağı	*a-yak-kabuh ba:uh*
ladies'	bayanlar tuvaleti	*ba-yanlaR too-aleti*
lake	göl	*gurl*
lamp	lamba	*lamba*
land	inmek	*inmek*
lane	şerit	*sheRit*
language	dil	*dil*
large	büyük	*bewyewk*
last	geçen	*gechen*
last	son	*son*
last night	dün gece	*dewn gejeh*
late	geç	*gech*
later	sonra	*sonRa*
latest, at the	en son	*en son*
laugh	gülmek	*gewlmek*
launderette	çamaşırhane	*chamashuhR-haneh*
law	hukuk	*hookook*
laxative	müshil ilacı	*mews-hil ilajuh*
leak	sızıntı	*suhzuhntuh*
leather	deri	*deRi*
leather goods	deri mamülleri	*deRi mamewl-leRi*
leave	yola çıkmak	*yola chuhkmak*
leek	pırasa	*puhRasa*
left	sol	*sol*
left luggage	emanet	*ema**hn**et*
left, to the	sola	*sola*
leg	bacak	*bajak*
lemon	limon	*limon*
lend	borç vermek	*boRch veRmek*
lens	mercek	*meRjek*
lentils	mercimek	*meRjimek*
less	daha az	*da-ha az*
lesson	ders	*deRs*
letter	mektup	*mektoop*

lettuce	marul	*maRool*
level crossing	hemzemin geçit	*hemzemin gechit*
library	kütüphane	*kewtewp-haneh*
lie	uzanmak	*oozanmak*
lies, to tell	yalan söylemek	*yalan suhylemek*
lift (hitchhike)	otostop	*otostop*
lift (in building)	asansör	*asansurR*
lift (ski)	telesiyej	*telesiyezh*
light (not dark)	aydınlık	*íduhnluhk*
light (not heavy)	hafif	*hafif*
light	lamba	*lamba*
lighter (cigarette)	çakmak	*chakmak*
lighthouse	fener	*feneR*
lightning	şimşek	*shimshek*
like (verb)	hoşlanmak, sevmek	*hoshlanmak, sevmek*
line	çizgi	*chizgi*
linen	keten	*keten*
lipstick	ruj	*roozh*
liqueur	likör	*likuhR*
liquid gas	likit gaz	*likit gaz*
listen	dinlemek	*dinlemek*
literature	edebiyat	*edebiyat*
litre	litre	*litReh*
little	az	*az*
little (a)	biraz	*biRaz*
live	oturmak	*otooRmak*
live together	beraber yaşamak	*beRabeR yashamak*
lobster	istakoz	*istakoz*
local	lokal	*lokal*
lock	kilit	*kilit*
long	uzun	*oozoon*
look	bakmak	*bakmak*
look for	aramak	*aRamak*
look up (in dictionary)	aramak	*aRamak*
lorry	kamyon	*kam-yon*
lose	kaybetmek	*kíbetmek*

loss	kayıp	*kí-uhp*
lost	kayıp	*kí-uhp*
lost item	kayıp eşya	*kí-uhp eshya*
lost property office	kayıp eşya bürosu	*kí-uhp eshya bewRosoo*
lost, to be	kaybolmak	*kaybolmak*
lotion	losyon	*losyon*
loud	gürültülü, yüksek sesli	*gewRewltewlew, yewksek sesli*
love (verb)	sevmek	*sevmek*
love	sevgi (aşk)	*sevgi (ashk)*
love, be in – with	-e aşık olmak	*-eh ashuhk olmak*
low	alçak	*alchak*
low tide	alçak gel-git	*alchak gel-git*
luck	şans	*shans*
luggage	bagaj	*bagazh*
luggage locker	bagaj dolabı	*bagazh dolabuh*
lunch	öğle yemeği	*ur:leh yeme:i*
lunchroom	yemek salonu	*yemek salonoo*
lungs	akciğer	*akji:eR*

M

macaroni	makarna	*makaRna*
madam	bayan	*ba-yan*
magazine	dergi	*deRgi*
mail	posta	*posta*
main post office	merkez postane	*meRkez postaneh*
main road	ana yol	*ana yol*
make an appointment	randevu almak	*randevoo almak*
make love	sevişmek	*sevishmek*
makeshift	geçici	*gechiji*
man	erkek	*eRkek*
manager	müdür	*mewdewR*
mandarin	mandalina	*mandalina*
manicure	manikür	*manikewR*
map	harita	*haRita*

marble	mermer	*meRmeR*
March	mart	*maRt*
margarine	margarin	*maRgaRin*
marina	yat limanı	*yat limanuh*
market	pazar	*pazaR*
marriage	evlilik	*evlilik*
married	evli	*evli*
married, get	evlenmek	*evlenmek*
massage	masaj	*masazh*
mat	mat	*mat*
match	maç	*mach*
matches	kibrit	*kibRit*
May	mayıs	*ma-yuhs*
maybe	belki	*belki*
mayonnaise	mayonez	*ma-yonez*
mayor	belediye başkanı	*belediyeh bashkanuh*
meal	yemek	*yemek*
mean	...anlamına gelmek	*...anlamuhna gelmek*
meat	et	*et*
medication	ilaç	*ilach*
medicine	ilaç	*ilach*
meet	tanışmak	*tanuhshmak*
melon	karpuz; kavun	*kaRpooz, kavoon*
membership	üyelik	*ew-yelik*
menstruate	adet görmek	*adet gurRmek*
menstruation	adet kanaması	*adet kanamasuh*
menu	menü	*menew*
menu of the day	günün menüsü	*gewnewn menewsew*
message	mesaj, not	*mesazh, not*
metal	metal	*metal*
meter	taksimetre	*taksimetReh*
metre	metre	*metReh*
migraine	migren	*migRen*
mild (tobacco)	hafif	*hafif*
milk	süt	*sewt*
millimetre	milimetre	*milimetReh*
milometer	kilometre sayacı	*kilometReh sa-yajuh*

minaret	minare	*minaReh*
mince	kıyma	*kuhyma*
mineral water	maden suyu	*maden soo-yoo*
minute	dakika	*dakika*
mirror	ayna	*ína*
miss	özlemek	*urzlemek*
missing person	kayıp kişi	*ka-yuhp kishi*
missing, to be	kayıp olmak	*ka-yuhp olmak*
mistake	yanlışlık	*yanluhshluhk*
mistaken, to be	yanılmak	*yanuhlmak*
misunderstanding	yanlış anlama	*yanluhsh anlama*
mixture	şurup	*shooRoop*
mocha	yemen kahvesi	*yemen kaHvesi*
modern art	günümüz sanatı	*gewnewmewz sanatuh*
molar	azı (dişi)	*azuh (dishi)*
moment	saniye, an	**sah**niyeh, an
monastery	dergah	*deRgah*
Monday	pazartesi	*pazaRtesi*
money	para	*paRa*
month	ay	*í*
moped	mobilet	*mobilet*
morning, in the	sabahleyin	*sabaHleyin*
mosque	cami	*jami*
mosque prayers	namaz	*namaz*
motel	motel	*motel*
mother	anne	*an-neh*
motor cross	motokros	*moto-kRos*
motorbike	motosiklet	*motosiklet*
motorboat	deniz motoru	*deniz motoRoo*
motorway	otoyol	*oto-yol*
mountain	dağ	*da:*
mountain hut	dağ kulübesi	*da: koolewbesi*
mountaineering	dağcılık sporu	*da:juhluhk spoRoo*
mountaineering shoes	dağcılık ayakkabıları	*da:juhluhk a-yak-kabuhlaRuh*
mouse	fare	*faReh*
mouth	ağız	*a:uhz*

much/many	çok	chok
multistorey car park	çok katlı otopark	chok katluh otopaRk
muscle	kas	kas
muscle spasms	kas kasılması	kas kasuhlmasuh
museum	müze	mewzeh
mushrooms	mantar	mantaR
music	müzik	mewzik
musical	müzikal	mewzikal
mussels	midye	mid-yeh
mustard	hardal	haRdal

N

nail (finger)	tırnak	turRnak
nail	çivi	chivi
nail polish	oje	ozheh
nail polish remover	aseton	aseton
nail scissors	tırnak makası	turRak makasuh
naked	çıplak	chuhplak
nappy	çocuk bezi	chojook bezi
National Health	sosyal sigorta	sosyal sigoRta
	kurumu	kooRoomoo
nationality	uyruk	uyRook
natural	doğal	do:al
nature	doğa	do:a
naturism	doğacılık	do:ajuhluhk
nausea	mide bulantısı	mideh boolantuhsuh
near	...yakın	...yakuhn
nearby	yakın	yakuhn
necessary	gerekli	geRekli
neck	boyun	boyoon
necklace	kolye	kol-yeh
nectarine	tüysüz şeftali	tewysewz sheftali
needle	iğne	i:neh
negative	negatif	negatif
neighbours	komşular	komshoolaR
nephew	yeğen (erkek)	ye:en (eRkek)

never	asla	asla
new	yeni	yeni
news	haberler	habeRleR
news stand	gazete bayisi	gazeteh bí-isi
newspaper	gazete	gazeteh
next	gelecek	gelejek
next to	...yanında	...yanuhnda
nice (friendly)	cana yakın	jana yakuhn
nice (to the eye)	hoş	hosh
nice (tasty)	lezzetli	lez-zetli
niece	yeğen (kız)	ye:en (kuhz)
night	gece	gejeh
night duty	gece nöbeti	gejeh nurbeti
nightclub	gece kulübü	gejeh koolewbew
nightlife	gece hayatı	gejeh ha-yatuh
no one	hiç kimse	hich kimseh
no	hayır	ha-yuhR
no overtaking	geçme yasağı	gechmeh yasa:uh
noise	gürültü	gewRewltew
nonstop	duraklamadan	dooRaklamadan
normal	normal	noRmal
north	kuzey	koozey
nose	burun	booRoon
nose drops	burun damlası	booRoon damlasuh
nosebleed	burun kanaması	booRoon kanamasuh
notepaper	dosya kağıdı	dosya ka:uhduh
nothing	hiç bir şey	hich biR shey
November	kasım	kasuhm
nowhere	hiç bir yerde	hich biR yeRdeh
nudist beach	çıplaklar plajı	chuhplaklaR plazhuh
number	numara	noomaRa
number plate	plaka	plaka
nurse	hemşire	hemshiReh
nutmeg	küçük hindistan cevizi	kewchewk hindistan jevizi
nuts	fındık fıstık	fuhnduhk fuhstuhk

O

October	ekim	*ekim*
off licence	tekel	*tekel*
off	bozuk	*bozook*
offer	ikram etmek	*ikRam etmek*
office	büro	*bewRo*
oil	yağ	*ya:*
oil level	yağ seviyesi	*ya: seviyesi*
ointment	merhem	*meRhem*
ointment for burns	yanık merhemi	*yanuhk meRhemi*
okay	tamam	*tamam*
old	yaşlı	*yashluh*
olive oil	zeytin yağı	*zeytin ya:uh*
olives	zeytin	*zeytin*
omelette	omlet	*omlet*
on	...üzerine; üzerinde	*...ewzeRindeh, ewzeRindeh*
on board	gemide	*gemideh*
on the way	yolda	*yolda*
oncoming car	karşı yönden gelen araba	*kaRshuh yurnden gelen aRaba*
one-way traffic	tek yönlü yol	*tek yurnlew yol*
onion	soğan	*so:an*
open	açık	*achuhk*
open	açmak	*achmak*
opera	opera	*opeRa*
operate	ameliyat etmek	*ameliyat etmek*
operator (telephone)	operatör	*opeRaturR*
operetta	operet	*opeRet*
opposite	karşısında	*kaRshuhsuhnda*
optician	gözlükçü	*gurzlewkchew*
orange	portakal rengi	*poRtakal rengi*
orange	portakal	*poRtakal*
orange juice	portakal suyu	*poRtakal soo-yoo*
order (in -, tidy)	yolunda (derli toplu)	*yoloonda (deRli toploo)*
order	sipariş	*sipaRish*

order (verb)	ısmarlamak	*uhsmaRlamak*
other	başka	*bashka*
other side	karşı taraf	*kaRshuh taRaf*
outside	...dışında	*...duhshuhnda*
overtake	geçmek	*gechmek*
oysters	istiridye	*istiRid-yeh*

p

packed lunch	hazır öğle yemeği paketi	*hazuhR ur:leh yeme:i paketi*
page	sayfa	*sífa*
pain	ağrı	*a:Ruh*
painkiller	ağrı kesici	*a:Ruh kesiji*
paint	boya	*boya*
painting (art)	ressamlık	*res-samluhk*
painting (object)	resim	*resim*
palace	saray	*saRí*
pan	tencere	*tenjeReh*
pancake	krep süzet	*kRep sewzet*
pane	cam	*jam*
pants	pantalon	*pantalon*
panty liner	ped	*ped*
paper	kağıt	*ka:uht*
paprika	kırmızı biber	*kuhrRmuhzuh bibeR*
paraffin oil	gaz yağı	*gaz ya:uh*
parasol	güneşten koruyan şemsiye	*gewneshten koRooyan shemsiyeh*
parcel	paket	*paket*
pardon	pardon	*paRdon*
parents	anne ve baba	*an-neh veh baba*
park	park	*paRk*
park	park etmek	*paRk etmek*
parking space	park yeri	*paRk yeRi*
parsley	maydanoz	*mídanoz*
part	yedek parça	*yedek paRcha*
partner	eş	*esh*

party	parti	*paRti*
passable	geçilir	*gechiliR*
passenger	yolcu	*yoljoo*
passport	pasaport	*pasapoRt*
passport photo	vesikalık fotğraf	*vesikaluhk foto:Raf*
patient	hasta	*hasta*
pavement	kaldırım	*kalduhRuhm*
pay	ödemek	*urdemek*
pay the bill	hesabı ödemek	*hesabuh urdemek*
peach	şeftali	*sheftali*
peanuts	fıstık	*fuhstuhk*
pear	armut	*aRmoot*
peas	bezelye	*bezel-yeh*
pedal	pedal	*pedal*
pedestrian crossing	yaya geçidi	*ya-ya gechidi*
pedicure	pedikür	*pedikewR*
pen	kalem	*kalem*
pencil	kurşun kalem	*kooRshoon kalem*
penis	penis	*penis*
pepper	biber	*bibeR*
performance	gösteri	*gursteRi*
perfume	parfüm	*paRfewm*
perm (verb)	perma yapmak	*peRma yapmak*
perm	perma	*peRma*
permit	ruhsat	*rooHsat*
person	kişi	*kishi*
personal	kişisel	*kishisel*
petrol	benzin	*benzin*
petrol station	benzin istasyonu	*benzin istas-yonoo*
pets	ev hayvanları	*ev hívanlaRuh*
pharmacy	eczane	*ejzaneh*
phone (verb)	telefon etmek	*elefon etmek*
phone	telefon	*telefon*
phone box	telefon kulübesi	*telefon koolewbesi*
phone directory	telefon rehberi	*telefon reHbeRi*
phone number	telefon numaras	*telefon noomaRasuh*
photo	fotoğraf, resim	*foto:Raf, resim*

photocopier	fotokopi makinesi	*fotokopi makinesi*
photocopy (verb)	fotokopi çekmek	*fotokopi chekmek*
photocopy	fotokopi	*fotokopi*
pick up	almak	*almak*
picnic	piknik	*piknik*
piece of clothing	giyecek	*giyejek*
pier	iskele	*iskeleh*
pigeon	güvercin	*gewveRjin*
pill (contraceptive)	doğum kontrol hapı	*do:oom kontRol hapuh*
pillow	yastık	*yastuhk*
pillowcase	yastık yüzü	*yastuhk yewzew*
pin	iğne	*i:neh*
pineapple	ananas	*ananas*
pipe	pipo	*pipo*
pipe tobacco	pipo tütünü	*pipo tewtewnew*
pity	yazık	*yazuhk*
place of entertainment	eğlence yeri	*e:lenjeh yeRi*
place of interest	görülmeye değer	*gurRewlmeyeh de:eR*
plan	plan	*plan*
plant	bitki	*bitki*
plasters	yara bandı	*yaRa banduh*
plastic	plastik	*plastik*
plastic bag	naylon torba	*nílon toRba*
plate	tabela	*tabela*
platform	peron	*peRon*
play (theatre)	piyes	*pi-yes*
play	oynamak	*oynamak*
play basketball	basketbol oynamak	*basketbol oynamak*
play golf	golf oynamak	*golf oynamak*
play tennis	tenis oynamak	*tenis oynamak*
playground	çocuk bahçesi	*chojook baHchesi*
playing cards	iskambil kağıtları	*iskambil ka:uhtlaruh*
pleasant	hoş	*hosh*
please	lütfen	*lewtfen*
pleasure	zevk	*zevk*
plum	erik	*eRik*

pocket knife	çakı	*chakuh*
point	göstermek	*gursteRmek*
poison	zehir	*ze-hiR*
police	polis	*polis*
police station	karakol	*kaRakol*
policeman	polis memuru	*polis memooRoo*
pond	gölet	*gurlet*
pony	midilli	*midil-li*
pop concert	pop konseri	*pop konseRi*
population	nüçus	*newfoos*
port	porto şarabı	*poRto shaRabuh*
porter	hamal	*hamal*
porter	kapıcı	*kapuhjuh*
post code	posta kodu	*post kodoo*
post office	postane	*postaneh*
postage	posta ücreti	*posta ewjReti*
postbox	posta kutusu	*posta kootoosoo*
postcard	kartpostal	*kaRtpostal*
postman	postacı	*postajuh*
potato	patates	*patates*
poultry	kümes hayvanları	*kewmes hívanlaRuh*
powdered milk	süt tozu	*sewt tozoo*
power point	priz	*pRiz*
pram	çocuk arabası	*chojook aRabasuh*
prawns	karides	*kaRides*
precious	değerli	*de:eRli*
prefer	tercih etmek	*teRji-h-etmek*
preference	tercih	*teRjih*
pregnant	hamile	*hahmileh*
present (available)	mevcut	*mevjoot*
present	hediye	*hediyeh*
press	basmak	*basmak*
pressure	basınç	*basuhnch*
price	fiyat	*fiyat*
price list	fiyat listesi	*fiyat listesi*
print (verb)	basmak	*basmak*

probably	büyük bir olasılıkla	*bewyewk biR olasuhluhkla*
problem	sorun	*soRoon*
profession	meslek	*meslek*
programme	program	*pRogRam*
pronounce	telaffuz etmek	*telaf-fooz etmek*
propane camping gas	propan kamp gazı	*pRopan kamp gazuh*
prune	kuru erik	*kooRoo eRik*
pudding	tatlı	*tatluh*
pull	çekmek	*chekmek*
pulled muscle	kas kopması	*kas kopmasuh*
pure	saf	*saf*
purple	mor	*moR*
purse	para cüzdanı	*paRa jewzdanuh*
push	itmek	*itmek*
puzzle	bulmaca	*boolmaja*
pyjamas	pijama	*pizhama*

Q

quarter	dörtte biri	*durRt-teh biRi*
quarter of an hour	on beş dakika	*on besh dakika*
queen	kraliçe	*kRalicheh*
question	soru	*soRoo*
quick	çabuk	*chabook*
quiet	sakin	*sakin*

R

radio	radyo	*radyo*
railways	demiryolu işletmesi	*demiR-yoloo ishletmesi*
rain (verb)	yağmur yağmak	*ya:mooR ya:mak*
rain	yağmur	*ya:mooR*
raincoat	yağmurluk	*ya:mooRlook*
raisins	kuru üzüm	*kooRoo ewzewm*
rape	tecavüz	*tejavewz*

rapids	hızlı akıntı yeri	*huhzluh akuhntuh yeRi*
raspberries	ahududu	*ahoodoodoo*
raw	çiğ	*chi:*
raw vegetables	çiğ sebze	*chi: sebzeh*
razor blades	jilet	*zhilet*
read	kitap okumak	*kitap okoomak*
ready	hazır	*hazuhR*
really	aslında	*asluhnda*
receipt	makbuz	*makbooz*
recipe	yemek tarifi	*yemek taRifi*
reclining chair	şezlong	*shezlong*
recommend	tavsiye etmek	*tavsiyeh etmek*
recovery service	TTOK	*teh teh o keh*
rectangle	dikdörtgen	*dikdurRtgen*
red	kırmızı	*kuhRmuhzuh*
red wine	kırmızı şarap	*kuhRmuhzuh shaRap*
reduction	indirim	*indiRim*
refrigerator	buzdolabı	*boozdolabuh*
regards	selamlar	*selamlaR*
region	bölge	*burlgeh*
registered (letter)	iadeli taahhütlü	*iahdeli tah-hewtlew*
registration	kayıt	*ka-yuht*
relatives	aile, akraba	*îleh, akRaba*
reliable	güvenilir	*gewveniliR*
religion	din	*din*
rent out	kiraya vermek	*kiRa-ya veRmek*
repair (verb)	tamir etmek	**tah***miR etmek*
repairs	tamir	**tah***miR*
repeat	tekrar etmek	*tekRaR etmek*
report	rapor	*rapoR*
resent	içerlemek	*icheRlemek*
responsible	sorumlu	*soRoomloo*
rest	dinlenmek	*dinlenmek*
restaurant	restoran	*restoRan*
result	sonuç	*sonooch*
retired	emekli	*emekli*
return (ticket)	gidiş dönüş	*gidish durnewsh*

reverse (vehicle)	geri yürütmek	geRi yewRewtmek
rheumatism	romatizma	romatizma
rice	pılav	puhlow
ridiculous	gülünç	gewlewnch
riding (horseback)	ata binmek	ata binmek
riding school	binicilik okulu	binijilik okooloo
right	sağ	sa:
right of way	öncelik	urnjelik
right, on the	sağa	sa:a
ripe	olgun	olgoon
risk	risk	risk
river	nehir, ırmak	ne-hiR, uhRmak
road	yol	yol
roadway	şose	shoseh
roasted	kavrulmuş	kavRoolmoosh
rock	kaya	ka-ya
roll	ufak ekmek	oofak ekmek
rolling tobacco	tütün	tewtewn (saRma
	(sarma sigara için)	sigaRa ichin)
roof rack	araba üst bagajı	aRaba ewst bagazhuh
room	oda	oda
room number	oda numarası	oda noomaRasuh
room service	oda servisi	oda seRvisi
rope	halat	halat
rosé	pembe şarap	pembeh shaRap
roundabout	dönel kavşak	durnel kavshak
route	yol	yol
rowing boat	sandal	sandal
rubber	lastik	lastik
rubbish	saçmalık	sachmaluhk
rucksack	küçük sırt çantası	kewchewk suhRt
		chantasuh
rude	kaba	kaba
ruins	harabe	haRabeh
run into	karşılaşmak	kaRshuhlashmak

sad	üzgün	*ewzgewn*
safari	safari	*safaRi*
safe	emin	*emin*
safe	kasa	*kasa*
safety pin	çengelli iğne	*chengel-li i:neh*
sail	yelken açmak	*yelken achmak*
sailing boat	yelkenli	*yelkenli*
salad	salata	*salata*
salad oil	zeytinyağı	*zeytin-ya:uh*
salami	salam	*salam*
sale	indirimli satışlar	*indiRimli satuhshlaR*
salt	tuz	*tooz*
same	aynısı	*ínuhsuh*
sandy beach	kumsal	*koomsal*
sanitary pad	ped	*ped*
sardines	sardalya	*saRdalya*
satisfied	memnun	*memnoon*
Saturday	cumartesi	*joomaRtesi*
sauce	sos	*sos*
sauna	sauna	*saoona*
sausage	sosis	*sosis*
savoury	tatlı olmayan	*tatluh olma-yan*
say	söylemek	*suhylemek*
say one's farewells	vedalaşmak	*vedalashmak*
scarf	eşarp, fular	*eshaRp, foolaR*
scenic walk	manzaralı gezinti	*manzaRuhluh gezinti*
school	okul	*okool*
scissors	makas	*makas*
scooter	skuter	*skooteR*
scorpion	akrep	*akRep*
screw	vida	*vida*
screwdriver	tornavida	*toRnavida*
sculpture	heykeltıraşlık	*heykeltuhRashluhk*
sea	deniz	*deniz*
seasick (to be)	deniz tutmak	*deniz tootmak*

seat	yer	yeR
secondhand	elden düşme	elden dewshmeh
second	saniye	sahniyeh
second	ikinci	ikinji
sedative	sakinleştirici hap	sakinleshtiRiji hap
see	görmek	gurRmek
self timer	otomatik deklanşör	otomatik deklanchurR
send	yollamak	yol-lamak
sentence	cümle	jewmleh
September	eylül	eylewl
serious	ciddi	jid-di
service	servis	seRvis
serviette	peçete	pecheteh
set (ladies' hair)	öndüle yapmak	urndewleh yapmak
sewing thread	iplik	iplik
shade	gölge	gurlgeh
shallow	sığ	suh:
shammy	güderi	gewdeRi
shampoo	şampuan	shampooan
shark	köpek balığı	kurpek baluh:uh
shave (verb)	tıraş olmak	tuhRash olmak
shaver	tıraş makinesi	tuhRash makinesi
shaving brush	tıraş fırçası	tuhRash fuhRchasuh
shaving cream	tıraş kremi	tuhRas kRemi
shaving soap	tıraş sabunu	tuhRash saboonoo
sheet	çarşaf	chaRshaf
sherry	şeri	sheRi
shirt	gömlek	gurmlek
shoe	ayakkabı	a-yak-kabuh
shoe polish	ayakkabı boyası	a-yak-kabuh boyasuh
shoe shop	ayakkabı mağazası	a-yak-kabuh ma:azasuh
shoemaker	kunduracı	koondooRajuh
shop	dükkan	dewk-kahn
shop (verb)	alış veriş yapmak	aluhsh veRish yapmak
shop assistant	tezgahtar	tezgahHtaR
shop window	vitrin	vitRin
shopping centre	alış veriş merkezi	aluhsh veRish meRkezi

short	kısa	*kuhsa*
short circuit	kısa devre	*kuhsa devReh*
shorts	şort	*shoRt*
shoulder	omuz	*omooz*
show	gösteri	*gursteRi*
shower	duş	*doosh*
shutter	obtüratör	*obtewRaturR*
sieve	süzgeç	*sewzgech*
sign	imzalamak	*imzalamak*
signature	imza	*imza*
silence	sessizlik	*ses-sizlik*
silver	gümüş	*gewmews*
silverplated	gümüş kaplama	*gewmewsh kaplama*
simple	basit	*basit*
single (unmarried)	bekar	*bekahR*
single (one way)	tek gidiş	*tek gidish*
single (one person)	tek kişilik	*tek kishilik*
sir	bey	*bey*
sister	kızkardeş	*kuhzkaRdesh*
sit	oturmak	*otooRmak*
size	numara	*noomaRa*
ski	kayak yapmak	*kíyak mak*
ski boots	kayak ayakkabıları	*kíyak ayak-kabuhlRuh*
ski goggles	kayak gözlüğü	*kíyak gurzlew:ew*
ski instructor	kayak hocası	*kíyak hojasuh*
ski lessons/class	kayak dersi	*kíyak deRsi*
ski lift	telesiyej, teleferik	*telesiyezh, telefeRik*
ski pants	kayak pantalonu	*kíyak pantalonoo*
ski pass	kayak pasosu	*kíyak pasosoo*
ski slope	kayak pisti	*kíyak pisti*
ski stick	kayak değneği	*kíyak de:ne:i*
ski suit	kayak kıyafeti	*kíyak kuhyafeti*
ski wax	kayak çilası	*kíyak chilasuh*
skimmed milk	yağı alınmış süt	*ya:uh aluhnmuhsh sewt*
skin	cilt	*jilt*
skirt	etek	*etek*

skis	kayak	*kíak*
sleep	uyumak	*ooyoomak*
sleeping car	kuşetli vagon	*kooshetli vagon*
sleeping pills	uyku hapı	*ooykoo hapuh*
slide	slayt	*slít*
slip	jüpon	*jewpon*
slip road	tali yol	*tahli yol*
slow	yavaş	*yavash*
slow train	yolcu/posta treni	*yoljoo/posta tReni*
small	küçük	*kewchewk*
small change	bozuk para	*bozook paRa*
smell	kokmak	*kokmak*
smoke	duman	*dooman*
smoke	sigara içmek	*sigaRa ichmek*
smoked	füme	*fewmeh*
smoking compartment	sigara içilebilen vagon	*sigaRa ichilebilen vagon*
snake	yılan	*yuhlan*
snorkel	snorkel	*snoRkel*
snow (verb)	kar yağmak	*kaR ya:mak*
snow	kar	*kaR*
snow chains	araba zinciri	*aRaba zinjiRi*
soap	sabun	*saboon*
soap box	sabun kutusu	*saboon kootoosoo*
soap powder	çamaşır tozu	*chamashuhR tozoo*
soccer	futbol	*footbol*
soccer match	futbol maçı	*footbol machuh*
socket	priz	*pRiz*
socks	çorap	*choRap*
soft drink	meşrubat	*meshRoobat*
sole	taban	*taban*
sole (fish)	dil balığı	*dil baluh:uh*
solicitor	avukat	*avookat*
someone	biri	*biRi*
sometimes	bazen	*bazen*
somewhere	bir yerde	*biR yeRdeh*
son	oğul	*o:ool*

soon	biraz sonra	*biRaz sonRa*
sorbet	şerbet	*sheRbet*
sore	yara	*yaRa*
sore throat	boğaz ağrısı	*bo:az a:Ruhsuh*
sorry	özür dilerim	*urzewR diliRim*
sort	çeşit	*cheshit*
soup	çorba	*choRba*
sour	ekşi	*ekshi*
source	kaynak	*kínak*
south	güney	*gewney*
souvenir	hediyelik eşya	*hediyelik eshya*
spaghetti	spagetti	*spaget-ti*
spanner (open ended)	İngiliz anahtarı	*ingiliz anaHtaRuh*
spanner	cıvata anahtarı	*juhvata anaHtaRuh*
spare	yedek	*yedek*
spare parts	yedek parça	*yedek paRcha*
spare tyre	yedek lastik	*yedek lastik*
spare wheel	yedek tekerlek	*yedek tekeRlek*
speak	konuşmak	*konooshmak*
special	özel	*urzel*
specialist	uzman	*oozman*
speciality	spesiyalite	*spesiyaliteh*
speed limit	azami hız	*azami huhz*
spell	hecelemek	*hejelemek*
spicy	baharatlı	*ba-haRatluh*
splinter	kıymık	*kuhymuhk*
spoon	kaşık	*kashuhk*
spoonful	kaşık dolusu	*kashuhk doloosoo*
sport	spor	*spoR*
sports centre	spor merkezi	*spoR meRkezi*
spot	yer	*yeR*
sprain	burkmak	*booRkmak*
spring	ilkbahar	*ilkba-haR*
square	meydan	*meydan*
square (geometric)	kare	*kaReh*
square metres	metre kare	*metReh kaReh*
squash, to play	skuoş oynamak	*skoo-osh oynamak*

stadium	stadyum	stad-yoom
stain	leke	lekeh
stain remover	leke giderici	lekeh gideRiji
stairs	merdiven	meRdiven
stalls	salon	salon
stamp	posta pulu	posta pooloo
start	çalıştırmak	chaluhshtuhRmak
station	istasyon	istasyon
statue	heykel	heykel
stay (verb)	kalmak	kalmak
stay	zaman	zaman
steal	çalmak	chalmak
steel	çelik	chelik
stench	pis koku	pis kokoo
sting (insect only)	ısırmak	uhsuhRmak
stitch (med.)	dikiş	dikish
stitch (verb)	dikmek	dikmek
stock	et suyu	et soo-yoo
stockings	çorap	choRap
stomach	mide	mideh
stomach ache	mide ağrısı	mideh a:Ruhsuh
stomach cramps	karın spazmi	kaRuhn spazmi
stools	dışkı	dushkuh
stop (verb)	durmak	dooRmak
stop	durak	dooRak
stopover	aktarma	aktaRma
storm	fırtına	fuhRtuhna
straight	doğru	do:Roo
straight ahead	doğru	do:Roo
straw	kamış	kamuhsh
strawberries	çilek	chilek
street	sokak	sokak
street side	sokağa bakan	soka:a bakan
strike	grev	gRev
strong (tea)	demli	demli
study	okumak	okoomak
stuffing	içi	ichi

subscriber's number	abone telefon numarası	*aboneh telefon noomaRasuh*
subtitled	alt yazılı	*alt yazuhluh*
succeed	başarmak	*bashaRmak*
sugar	şeker	*shekeR*
sugar lumps	kesmeşeker	*kesmeshekeR*
suit	takım elbise	*takuhm elbiseh*
suitcase	bavul, valiz	*bavool, valiz*
summer	yaz	*yaz*
summertime	yaz mevsimi	*yaz mevsimi*
sun	güneş	*gewnesh*
sun hat	güneş şapkası	*gewnesh shapkasuh*
sunbathe	güneşlenmek	*gewneshlenmek*
Sunday	pazar	*pazaR*
sunglasses	güneş gözlüğü	*gewnesh gurzlew:ew*
sunrise	gün doğması	*gewn do:masuh*
sunset	gün batımı	*gewn batımı*
sunstroke	güneş çarpması	*gewnesh chaRpmasuh*
suntan lotion	güneş kremi	*gewnesh kRemi*
suntan oil	güneş yağı	*gewnesh ya:uh*
supermarket	süpermarket	*sewpeRmaRket*
surcharge	ek	*ek*
surf	sörf yapmak	*surRf yapmak*
surf board	sörf kayağı	*surf ka-ya:uh*
surgery	muayene odası	*moo-a-yeneh odasuh*
surname	soyadı	*soyaduh*
surprise	sürpriz	*sewRpriz*
swallow	yutmak	*yootmak*
swamp	bataklık	*batakluhk*
sweat	ter	*teR*
sweet (charming)	şekerli	*shekeRli*
sweet (pudding)	şirin	*shiRin*
sweet	tatlı	*tatluh*
sweet corn	mısır	*muhsuhR*
sweeteners	tatlılaştırıcı	*tatlulashtuhRuhjuh*
sweets	şekerleme	*shekeRlemeh*
swim	yüzmek	*yewzmek*

swimming pool	yüzme havuzu	*yewzmeh havoozoo*
swimming trunks	mayo	*ma-yo*
swindle	dolandırıcılık	*dolanduhRuhjuhluhk*
switch	şalter	*shalteR*
synagogue	sinagog	*sinagog*

T

table	masa	*masa*
table tennis (to play)	masa tenisi oynamak	*masa tenisi oynamak*
tablet	ilaç tableti	*ilach tableti*
take	almak	*almak*
take pictures	fotoğraf çekmek	*foto:Raf chekmek*
taken	dolu	*doloo*
talcum powder	talk pudrası	*talk poodRasuh*
talk	konuşmak	*konooshmak*
tall	uzun boylu	*oozoon boyloo*
tampons	tamponlar	*tamponlaR*
tanned	bronzlaşmış	*bRonzlashmuhsh*
tap	musluk	*mooslook*
tap water	musluk suyu	*mooslook soo-yoo*
taste	güzel zevk	*gewzel zevk*
tax free shop	gümrüksüz mağaza	*gewmRewksewz ma:aza*
taxi	taksi	*taksi*
taxi stand	taksi durağı	*taksi dooRa:uh*
tea	çay	*chí*
teapot	çaydanlık	*chídanluhk*
teaspoon	çay kaşığı	*chí kashuh:uh*
teat (baby's bottle)	plastik meme	*plastik memeh*
telegram	telgraf	*telegRaf*
telephoto lens	teleobjektif	*tele-obzhektif*
television	televizyon	*televizyon*
telex	teleks	*teleks*
temperature	sıcaklık	*suhjakluhk*
temporary filling	geçici dolgu	*gechiji dolgoo*

tender	yumuşak	*yoomooshak*
tennis ball	tenis topu	*tenis topoo*
tennis court	tenis kortu	*tenis koRtoo*
tennis racket	tenis raketi	*tenis raketi*
tenpin bowling	bovling	*bohling*
tent	çadır	*chaduhR*
tent peg	çadır kazığı	*chaduhR kazuh:uh*
terrace	teras	*teRas*
terribly	müthiş	*mewt-hish*
thank	teşekkür etmek	*teshek-kewR etmek*
thank you	teşekkür ederim	*teshek-kewR edeRim*
thanks	teşekkürler	*teshek-kewRleR*
thaw	erimek	*eRimek*
theatre	tiyatro	*tiyatRo*
theft	hırsızlık	*huhRsuhzluhk*
there	orada	*oRada*
thermal bath	kaplıca	*kapluhja*
thermometer	termometre	*teRmometReh*
thick	kalın	*kaluhn*
thief	hırsız	*huhRsuhz*
thigh	üst bacak	*ewst bajak*
thin	ince	*injeh*
things	eşya	*eshya*
think	düşünmek	*dewshewnmek*
third	üçte biri	*ewchteh biRi*
thirsty, to be	susamış olmak	*soosamuhsh olmak*
this afternoon	bugün öğleden sonra	*boogewn urleden sonRa*
this evening	bu akşam	*boo aksham*
this morning	bu sabah	*boo sabaH*
thread	iplik	*iplik*
throat	boğaz	*bo:az*
throat lozenges	pastil	*pastil*
throw up	kusmak	*koosmak*
thunderstorm	fırtına	*fuhRtuhna*
Thursday	perşembe	*peRshembeh*
ticket (admission)	bilet	*bilet*

ticket (travel)	bilet	*bilet*
tickets	biletler	*biletleR*
tidy (verb)	toplamak	*toplamak*
tie	kravat	*kRavat*
tights	külotlu çorap	*kewlotloo choRap*
time	zaman	*zaman*
times	kere, defa	*keReh, defa*
timetable	tarife	*taRifeh*
tin	konserve	*konseRveh*
tip	bahşiş	*baH-shish*
tissues	kağıt mendil	*ka:uht mendil*
toast	kızarmış ekmek	*kuhzaRmuhsh ekmek*
tobacco	tütün	*tewtewn*
toboggan	kızak	*kuhzak*
today	bugün	*boogewn*
toe	ayak parmağı	*a-yak paRma:uh*
together	beraber	*beRabeR*
toilet	tuvalet	*too-alet*
toilet paper	tuvalet kağıdı	*too-alet ka:uhduh*
toilet seat	tuvalet oturağı	*too-alet otooRa:uh*
toiletries	kozmetik malzemeleri	*kozmetik malzemeleRi*
tomato	domates	*domates*
tomato purée	domates salçası	*domates salchasuh*
tomato sauce	domates sosu	*domates sosoo*
tomorrow	yarın	*yaRuhn*
tongue	dil	*dil*
tonic water	tonik	*tonik*
tonight	bu gece	*boo gejeh*
too much	fazla	*fazla*
tools	araç gereç	*aRach geRech*
tooth	diş	*dish*
toothache	diş ağrısı	*dish a:Ruhsuh*
toothbrush	diş fırçası	*dish fuhRchasuh*
toothpaste	diş macunu	*dish majoonoo*
toothpick	kürdan	*kewRdan*
top up	doldurmak	*doldooRmak*

total	toplam	*toplam*
tough	sert	*seRt*
tour	tur	*tur*
tour guide	tur rehberi	*tooR reHbeRi*
tourist card	turist kartı	*tooRist kaRtuh*
tourist class	turistik sınıf	*tooRistik suhnuhf*
Tourist Information office	danışma bürosu	*danuhshma bewRosoo*
tourist menu	turistik menü	*tooRistik menew*
tow	çekmek	*chekmek*
tow cable	çekme halatı	*chekmeh halatuh*
towel	havlu	*havloo*
tower	kule	*kooleh*
town	kasaba	*kasaba*
town hall	belediye sarayı	*belediyeh saRí-uh*
toys	oyuncak	*oyoonjak*
traffic	trafik	*tRafik*
traffic light	trafik ışıkları	*tRafik uhshuhklaRuh*
trailer tent	açılır kapanır karavan	*achuhluhR kapanuhR kaRavan*
train	tren	*tRen*
train ticket	tren bileti	*tRen bileti*
train timetable	tren tarifesi	*tRen taRifesi*
training shoes	spor ayakkabısı	*spoR a-yak-kabuhsuh*
translate	tercüme etmek	*teRjewmeh etmek*
travel	seyahat etmek	*seya-hat etmek*
travel agent	seyahat acentası	*seya-hat ajentasuh*
travel guide	seyahat rehberi	*seya-hat reHbeRi*
traveller	yolcu	*yoljoo*
traveller's cheque	seyahat çeki	*seya-hat cheki*
treacle/syrup	şeker pekmezi/ şurup	*shekeR pekmezi/ shooRoop*
treatment	tedavi	*tedahvi*
triangle	üçgen	*ewchgen*
trim	ucundan almak	*oojoondan almak*
trip	gezi	*gezi*
trouble	şikayet	*shika-yet*

trout	alabalık	*alabaluhk*
trunk call	şehirlerarası	*she-hiRleRaRasuh*
	telefon konuşması	*telefon konooshmasuh*
trustworthy	güvenilir	*gewveniliR*
try on	denemek	*denemek*
tube	tüp	*tewp*
Tuesday	salı	*saluh*
tumble drier	çamaşır kurutma	*chamashuhR*
	makinesi	*kooRootma makinesi*
tuna	ton balığı	*ton baluh:uh*
tunnel	tünel	*tewnel*
Turkish	Türkçe	*tewRkcheh*
turn	sıra	*suhRa*
TV	televizyon	*televizyon*
TV guide	televizyon rehberi	*televizyon reHbeRi*
tweezers	cımbız	*juhmbuhz*
tyre	dış lastik	*duhsh lastik*
tyre lever	salapurya	*salapooR-ya*
tyre pressure	hava basıncı	*hava basuhnjuh*

U

ugly	çirkin	*chiRkin*
umbrella	şemsiye	*shemsiyeh*
under	...altında	*...altuhnda*
underground	metro	*metRo*
underground railway system	metro ağı	*metRo a:uh*
underground station	metro istasyonu	*metRo istasyonoo*
underpants	külot	*kewlot*
understand	anlamak	*anlamak*
underwear	iç çamaşırı	*ich chamashuhRuh*
undress	soyunmak	*soyoonmak*
unemployed	işsiz	*ishsiz*
uneven	pürüzlü	*pewRewzlew*
university	üniversite	*ewniveRsiteh*
210 unleaded	kurşunsuz benzin	*kooRshoonsooz benzin*

up	yukarı	yookaRuh
urgent	acil	ah-jil
urgently	acilen	ahjilen
urine	idrar	idRaR
usually	çoğunlukla	cho:oonlookla

V

vacate	boşaltmak	boshaltmak
vaccinate	aşılamak	ashuhlamak
vagina	vajina	vazhina
vaginal infection	vajinal enfeksiyon	vazhinal enfeksiyon
valid	geçerli	gecheRli
valley	vadi	vadi
valuable	değerli	de:eRli
van	kamyonet	kam-yonet
vanilla	vanilya	vanilya
vase	vazo	vazo
vaseline	vazelin	vazelin
veal	dana eti	dana eti
vegetable soup	sebze çorbası	sebzeh choRbasuh
vegetables	sebze	sebzeh
vegetarian	vejetaryen	vezhetaR-yen
vein	damar	damaR
(vending) machine	otomatik satış makinesi	otomatik satuhsh makinesi
venereal disease	cinsel hastalık	jinsel hastaluhk
via	...yoluyla	...yolooyla
video recorder	video	video
video tape	video kaseti	video kaseti
view	manzara	manzaRa
village	köy	kuhy
visa	vize	vizeh
visit	ziyaret etmek	ziyaRet etmek
vitamin tablets	vitamin hapları	vitamin haplaRuh
vitamins	vitamin	vitamin
volcano	yanardağ	yanaRda:

| volleyball | voleybol | *voleybol* |
| vomit | istifrağ etmek | *istifRa: etmek* |

W

wait	beklemek	*beklemek*
waiter	garson	*gaRson*
waiting room	bekleme odası	*beklemeh odasuh*
waitress	bayan garson	*ba-yan gaRson*
wake up	uyandırmak	*ooyanduhRmak*
walk	yürüşmek	*yewRewshmek*
walk	yürümek	*yewRewmek*
wallet	cüzdan	*jewzdan*
wardrobe	elbise dolabı	*elbiseh dolabuh*
warm	ılık	*uhluhk*
warn	uyarmak	*ooyaRmak*
warning	uyarı	*ooyaRuh*
wash	yıkamak	*yuhkamak*
washing powder	çamaşır tozu	*chamashuhR tozoo*
washing	çamaşır	*chamashuhR*
washing line	çamaşır ipi	*chamuhshuhR ipi*
washing machine	çamaşır makinesi	*chamashuhR makinesi*
wasp	eşek arısı	*eshek aRuhsuh*
watch	kol saati	*kol sahti*
water	su	*soo*
water ski	su kayağı yapmak	*soo ka-ya:uh yapmak*
waterproof	su geçirmez	*soo gechiRmez*
wavepool	suni dalgalı havuz	*sooni dalgaluh havooz*
way	yol	*yol*
we	biz	*biz*
weak (tea)	açık	*achuhk*
weather	hava	*hava*
weather forecast	hava raporu	*hava rapoRoo*
wedding	düğün	*dew:ewn*
Wednesday	çarşamba	*chaRshamba*
week	hafta	*hafta*
weekend	hafta sonu	*hafta sonoo*

weekend duty	hafta sonu nöbeti	*hafta sonoo nurbeti*
weekly ticket	haftalık abone bileti	*haftaluhk aboneh bileti*
welcome	hoş geldiniz	*hosh geldiniz*
well	iyi	*iyi*
west	batı	*batuh*
wet	ıslak	*ihslak*
wet (weather)	yağmurlu	*ya:mooRloo*
wetsuit	sörf kıyafeti	*surRf kuhyafeti*
what?	ne?	*neh?*
wheel	tekerlek	*tekeRlek*
wheelchair	tekerlekli sandalye	*tekeRlekli sandal-yeh*
when?	ne zaman?	*neh zaman?*
where?	nerede?	*neRedeh?*
which?	hangi?	*hangi?*
whipped cream	krem şanti	*kRem shanti*
white	beyaz	*beyaz*
white-haired	ak saçlı	*ak sachluh*
who?	kim?	*kim?*
wholemeal	kepekli	*kepekli*
wholemeal bread	kepekli ekmek	*kepekli ekmek*
why?	niçin?	*nichin?*
wide angle lens	geniş açılı mercek	*genish achuhluh meRjek*
widow	dul	*dool*
widower	dul	*dool*
wife	eş	*esh*
wind	rüzgar	*rewzgaR*
windbreak	rüzgarlık	*rewzgaRluhk*
windmill	değirmen	*de:iRmen*
window	pencere	*penjeReh*
window (pay desk)	gişe, vezne	*gisheh, vezneh*
windscreen wiper	cam sileceği	*jam sileje:i*
wine	şarap	*shaRap*
wine glass	şarap bardağı	*shaRap baRda:uh*
wine list	şarap listesi	*shaRap listesi*
winter	kış	*kuhsh*
witness	görgü tanığı	*gurRgew tanuh:uh*

woman	kadın	*kaduhn*
wonderful	şahane	*sha-haneh*
wood	tahta	*taHta*
wool	yün	*yewn*
word	sözcük, kelime	*surzjewk, kelimeh*
work	iş	*ish*
working day	iş günü	*ish gewnew*
worn	aşınmış	*ashuhnmuhsh*
worried	endişeli	*endisheli*
wound	yara	*yaRa*
wrap	paketlemek	*paketlemek*
wrist	bilek	*bilek*
write	yazmak	*yazmak*
write down	not etmek	*not etmek*
writing pad	bloknot	*bloknot*
writing paper	dosya kağıdı	*dosya ka:uhduh*
written	yazılı	*yazuhluh*
wrong	yanlış	*yanluhsh*

Y

yacht	yat	*yat*
year	sene, yıl	*seneh, yuhl*
yellow	sarı	*saRuh*
yes	evet	*evet*
yes, please	lütfen	*lewtfen*
yesterday	dün	*dewn*
yoghurt	yoğurt	*yo:ooRt*
you	siz	*siz*
you too	size de	*sizeh deh*
youth hostel	gençlik yurdu	*genchlik yooRdoo*

Z

| zip | fermuar | *feRmooaR* |
| zoo | hayvanat bahçesi | *hívanat baHchesi* |

Basic grammar

1 The importance of suffixes, and their varying forms

A very distinctive feature of Turkish is the way it builds up
increasingly complex meanings from simple words. This is done with
suffixes – either in the middle of words or on the end. English, in
contrast, adds other, quite separate words for the same effect, eg:

gidiyorum   I am going
gitmiyorum   I am not going
gidebileceğim I will be able to go

However, these suffixes change their form to echo the vowels in the
particular words in which they occur. Plurals, for instance, can end in
-ler or **-lar**.

Another example is the 'detached' question suffix with four variants.
In the 'you' form, polite or plural, these are: **misiniz, mısınız, müsünüz**
and **musunuz**. Choosing the right one rapidly becomes instinctive,
but it is first necessary to understand what determines the variant.

2 Vowel harmony

Vowels are classed as front or back. Front vowels are **e, i, ö** and **ü**; back vowels are **a, ı, o** and **u**. A native Turkish word is made up solely of either front or back vowels (e.g. **güneşli**, sunny) – it never mixes front and back – and all suffixes must obey a similar harmony. The only exceptions are foreign loan words.

There are two typical variations of suffix harmony: in the first, all front vowels are echoed by **e**, and all back vowels by **a** (giving plurals **-ler** and **-lar**). In the second type, the last syllable in the root word is echoed, and this is how:
e and **i** are echoed by **i**
ö and **ü** by **ü**

a and **ı** by **ı**
o and **u** by **u**

These shape the question suffixes:

güzel mi?	is it beautiful?	**sütlü mü?**	is it milky?
kırmızı mı?	is it red?	**bozuk mu?**	is it broken?

They also shape the personal suffixes. After a consonant, and where the last vowel was **e** or **i** these are:
-im (my), **-in** (your), **-i** (his, hers, its),
-imiz (our) **-iniz** (polite 'your' singular, or 'your' plural) and **-leri** (their)

With **iş** (job) this gives:
işim (my job) **işin** (your job) **işi** (her job)
işimiz (our job) **işiniz** (your job) **işleri** (their job)

But the echo changes as the vowel changes: **buzum** – my ice (**buz** = ice), **gülün** – your rose (**gül** = rose) and **atı** – his horse (**at** = horse). Note that **-leri** is slightly different – it has only two forms. It is **-leri** for all front-vowel words, and **ları** for all back vowels.

3 The missing verbs: 'to be' and 'to have'

This is perhaps the moment to point out that there is no verb 'to have' in Turkish, nor is there a 'to be' either – or not in the present tense, at least. Instead another, slightly different set of suffixes is added to nouns or adjectives – again with the same four-fold echo. These are (after an **i** or **e**):

-(y)im – I am; **-sin** – you are; **-dir** (very often omitted) he, she it is; **-(y)iz** – we are; **-siniz** – you are (plural or polite form); **-(dir)ler** – they are.

Examples are:

iyiyim	(I am well)
iyisin	(you are well)
iyi misin?	(are you well?)

iyi (he, she is well), etc.
But the harmonising echoes also give:

Türksün	you are Turkish
kadınsın	you are a woman
adam mısın?	are you a man? and so on.

Two very useful words supplement these suffixes:

var (there is, there are) and **yok** (there is no, there are no).

Para var means there is money, and **para yok** means 'there is no money'.

But if the personal suffixes (see previous section) are combined with **para**, there is a complete change of meaning. The effect is the same as our verb 'to have'.

Param var means 'I have (some) money', and **param yok** is 'I have no money'. The same harmonising echoes recur: **arkadaşın** var (you have a friend), **sorunu** var (he, she has a problem) and then again **Çözümüz var** (we have a solution). (Root words are **arkadaş, sorun** and **çözüm.**)

4 Direct objects, 'to', 'from' and 'at'

The direct object of the sentence ('the man' in the sentence 'I saw the man') is modified in form if its English equivalent has the article 'the', 'my' (etc) or is a person's name, and not if it goes with 'a' or 'some'. The suffix which modifies the direct object has eight different variants **-(y)i**, **-(y)ı**, **-(y)ö**, or **-(y)u**.

Examples: **annemi gördüm** – I saw my mother (**anne** = mother); **Fatmayı gördüm** – I saw Fatma; but **bir kedi gördüm** – I saw a cat (**kedi** = cat). Note that the verb is at the end of the sentence, which is its normal position.

'To', 'from' and 'at' are expressed in Turkish with suffixes obeying the same two-fold -e/-a harmony mentioned above. Using **ey** (home/house) and **okul** (school):

eve = to home/the house   **okula** = to (the) school
evden = from home/the house   **okuldan** = from (the) school
evde = at home/the house   **okulda** = at (the) school

5 'You' - polite and familiar forms

Turkish is very like French, German and Italian in having polite and familiar forms of 'you' and 'your'. With people who know each other well, or are in informal situations, the familiar form is natural. If in any doubt, however, be polite.

6 More about verbs and tenses...

Here is another verb form using endings somewhat similar to those already illustrated for the present tense of 'to be'. It is shown with a front-vowel verb (**görmek** – to see) and a back-vowel verb (**yapmak** - to do).

The present continuous tense: 'I see/am seeing' – 'I do/am doing'

görüyorum	**görüyoruz**
yapıyorum	**yapıyoruz**
görüyorsun	**görüyorsunuz**
yapıyorsun	**yapıyorsunuz**
görüyor	**görüyorlar**
yapıyor	**yapıyorlar**

... and ever increasing complexities

Different suffixes provide all the different forms which verbs need to take; in every case the meaning is contained in a single word (except in the case of the detached question suffixes mentioned above).

Here are some examples:

-ecek/-acak	the future tense
-di, -dı, -dü, -du	the past tense
-meli/-malı	should or ought
-iyordu	past continuous
-ebil/-abi	I can, be able

eg (using **gelmek** to come) **gelecek** (he will come) **geldi** (he came) **gelmeli** (he ought to come) **geliyordu** (he was coming) **gelebilir** (he can or may come).

There are several combinations of tenses like -**iyordu**. One very useful such combination is the future-in-the-past -**ecekti** (the **d** of -**di** becomes a **t** in order to harmonise with the unvoiced **k**). It means 'I was going to'.

Others, much less commonly used, can give very subtle shades of meaning, such as 'I may not be able to', and 'I gather that I may not be able to'; there is even a tense with the meaning 'I am (quite) able not to' or 'it is possible that I am not' again using just a single word (eg **gelmiyebilirim**). But the beauty is that these complexities are built out of basic components and a remarkably simple logic.